Web Scripting in Windows (.NET)

Web Scripting in Windows (.NET)

William R. Champion

iUniverse, Inc.

New York Lincoln Shanghai

Web Scripting in Windows (.NET)

iUniverse, Inc.

For information address:
iUniverse, Inc.
2021 Pine Lake Road, Suite 100
Lincoln, NE 68512
www.iuniverse.com

ISBN: 0-595-29731-5

Printed in the United States of America

This book is dedicated to DeVry University, Irving, Texas, an environment that encouraged me to develop new techniques for my Computer Information System programming students.

Contents

Preface

You want to build Web Pages for use on The Internet, especially with Client-Server applications. This book introduces you to the fundamental Web software techniques, which expedites your learning Web Development software such as Macromedia DreamWeaver.

This textbook introduces the Reader to work with The Internet using HTML and scripting languages. HTML files are represented by Internet browsers as static WEB pages. Get more control over the appearance of Web pages with Cascading Style Sheets (CSS).

To add flexibility to WEB pages in HTML, use a scripting language to add program control to your WEB page. I start with JavaScript. An excellent use of a scripting language is to validate data locally before submitting the data to the Server Site. VBScript is relegated to Appendices A and B.

Client-Server is explored with Microsoft's Active Server Pages (ASP) and Sun Microsystems' Java Server Pages (JSP). JSP can run on Windows or Linux—multi-platform. The student is introduced to Microsoft's .NET platform.

While this isn't a book on Microsoft .NET, it examines ASP.NET and ADO.NET. I placed in Appendix C a FAQ (frequently asked questions) on Microsoft .NET (and Visual Studio .NET).

I learned this material by:

(1) reading books, making up and running my own examples, and using my material (with student handouts) in my DeVry programming classes in Visual Basic (HTML, JAVASCRIPT, ASP, ADO, XML), Java (JSP), and Macromedia DreamWeaver (HTML, CSS, JAVASCRIPT) over the last four years. To get into .NET I bought the software three years ago, several .NET books, and practiced with it.

(2) I attended appropriate seminars: last year on my sabbatical I attended a Microsoft .NET seminar in Orlando, Florida and Microsoft's "Boot Camp" on C#.

(3) An important resource was CDROM training courses in C#, .NET, and J2EE.

The unique aspects of this book:

(1) short, meaningful examples so the Reader can readily use the material for his own practice immediately;

(2) the chapters are self-contained, allowing you to work with only the chapters you are interested in.

Book Plan for Readers

Skip chapter 2 if you know HTML (including tables, lists, links, and forms).

Chapter 3 is an introduction for readers wanting more control over the visual appearance of their WEB pages.

Chapter 4 is for Readers interested in JavaScript. Appendices A and B use VBScript as the HTML scripting language.

Chapter 5 is for running Active Server Pages (ASP) and Active Data Objects (ADO) under Windows.

Chapter 6 gives you the alternatives of JScript, C#, and VB.NET scripting in WebPages running under the Microsoft .NET Platform.

Chapter 7 is for Readers who know the Java Programming Language and want to utilize Java Server Pages (JSP) on Windows.

Chapter 8 on XML is for everyone. Although Microsoft Access and MSDE (Microsoft Database Engine) are used by the Author, other ODBC-compatible databases (DB2, Oracle, SQL Server) can be utilized.

The Author's approach:

- Read what the concept is
- Try out the book's examples
- Change the examples to see if they still work
- Get creative with your ideas

It is not enough to read this material. First, run the book's examples. Then modify the examples and see if they still work. Finally, make up your own examples and test them. Email questions to: n1bonne1@bonnertx.com

Chapter 1

Web Pages and Scripting

1.0 Introduction to Web Pages

Web pages make up your Web Site. The basic way to set up a Web Page is to use HTML (Hypertext Protocol), a simple text language. Your editor could be Microsoft Notepad, Home Site, or Macromedia's DreamWeaver.

Chapter Two introduces the fundamentals of HTML, which could be skipped by knowledgeable Readers. HTML is used to set up the basic Web pages. Special attention is given to Forms, which gather information to be utilized in a Client-Server context.

Many Web users want more control over the appearance of their Web Pages. Chapter Three's Cascading Style Sheets (CSS) give more editorial and visual control (fonts, color, etc). This coding can be inserted into HTML documents. CSS Style Sheets can be externally saved and called from HTML pages.

A scripting language gives programming features, and can be inserted into HTML documents. JavaScript is a standardized Web scripting language which is multi-platform. If you use Microsoft's .NET platform, Microsoft's JScript runs JavaScript code without change.

Another scripting language is Microsoft's VBScript, a Visual BASIC look-alike. Since VBScript won't run in .NET, this material was placed in Appendices A and B.

Sun Microsystems Java Server Pages (JSP) is equivalent to Microsoft's ASP Web software. While JSP requires you to know Java as a scripting language, it runs under both Windows and Linux.

1.1 Microsoft Web Software

Web developers use Client-Server techniques to communicate between Server Sites and Local Sites. Microsoft Active Server Pages (ASP) serves this need well. ASP has an open architecture with a choice of VBScript or JavaScript scripting languages. The main text of this book covers JavaScript since it runs under .NET (unlike VBScript).

ASP.NET allows three scripting languages:

(1) JScript (runs JavaScript software)
(2) C# (with compilation)
(3) VB.NET (with compilation)

Microsoft's Active Data Objects (ADO) allows the use of databases (such as Microsoft's SQL Server, Microsoft's Access, or Oracle) in the Client-Server Web Environment. Why not store the database on the Web Server and let Local Sites access it through the Internet! ADO.NET carries this functionality to the .NET environment.

1.2 Java Server Pages

Java Server Pages (JSP) are the equivalent of Microsoft's Active server Pages (ASP). The scripting language is Java, with compilations.

Generally:

    (1) ASP is easier to use than JSP but not as efficient
    (2) JSP is harder to use than ASP but is more efficient
    (3) ASP only works under Windows while JSP can run under Windows or Linux.

You can buy packages that run ASP under Linux. But .NET platform may be positioned in the future to run under Linux! Web Services users may find it suitable to use both ASP and JSP, even in the same project!

1.3 Extended Modeling Language (XML)

XML is a standardized database language allowing communication over the Internet between unlike databases (such as Microsoft's SQL Server and Oracle).

XML is the brother of HTML:

> HTML: documents
> XML: data representation

Everybody likes XML for Internet communication: Microsoft, IBM. Oracle, etc. For example, Microsoft's Access 2003 Database stores its data in XML.

An introduction to XML's fundamentals is required for Internet Users, even those utilizing Mainframe IBM computers!

1.4 Summary

Learn how to set up Web Pages with HTML, and modify their contents with CSS.

Use scripting languages to run programming within your HTML pages, allowing you to validate data from a Form, and utilize Client-Server interactions between your Local Site and a Server Site over the Internet, including the use of a database on the Server. .

XML is the modern way of working with databases on The Web!

These fundamentals will allow you to delve into the depths of your programming specialization with more specific textbooks (or manuals)
later. See the Bibliography—and your local bookstore—for more
specialized books.

Plan which topics you will examine:

(1) Beginner in Internet on Windows: HTML, JavaScript, ASP, ADO

(2) Programmer who has used The Internet: CSS, JavaScript, ASP, ADO, XML

(3) Programmer who has used The Internet and is going to use Windows.NET: JavaScript, ASP, ADO, ASP.NET, ADO.NET, XML

(4) Java programmer who has used The Internet and is using Linux: JSP, XML

Chapter 2

HTML

2.0 Objectives

- Set up a HTML page with a Heading and a Body.

- Make the HTML page attractive visually.

- Insert graphic images in the HTML page.

- Represent data in an organized manner (tables, lists)

- Have clickable links to local and external WEB pages.

- Utilize Forms to accept data and initialize actions.

2.1 Introduction

HTML stands for Hypertext Transfer Language. It is the content of WEB pages run on Internet browsers such as Microsoft's Internet Explorer and Netscape's Navigator. HTML displays documents.

There are HTML editors available, some generating HTML segments, others based on working directly with HTML. You can use Microsoft's Notepad or a HTML editor, such as Allaire's Home Site.

It is important to know HTML even if you utilize a Web development system such as DreamWeaver. You need this knowledge to modify HTML code and know what the available choices are.

2.2 HTML Fundamentals

HTML (Hypertext Markup Language) sets up a WEB page to be run on a WEB browser. The Author uses Notepad as the editor, saving the file with the suffix .HTML.

The WEB page is remarked with the HTML tags:

```
<HTML>
……………..
</HTML>
```

Within these tags, distinguish between the HEAD (header) and the BODY (where most of the work is done):

```
<HTML>
<HEAD>
……..
</HEAD>

<BODY>
…………..
</BODY>
</HTML>
```

Note that predefined tags (HTML, HEAD, BODY) are used, with ending tags.

Each ending tag has a right-slash:

```
</HTML>
```

All these predefined tags could be all lower-case instead of all upper class.

In the HEAD you could add your TITLE:

```
<HEAD>
        <TITLE>MY GREAT PAGE!</TITLE>
</HEAD>
```

More will placed in the HEAD when we cover Cascading style Sheets (CSS) and scripts.

The BODY can contain:

- a message

- header size (H1, H2, H3, H4)

- spacing (BR for break to next line,

- P for paragraph skip two lines down,

- HR for horizontal line)

- font specifications

- keep the text as formatted (PRE for preformatted)

- tables (headings and details)

- lists (unordered and ordered)

- images

- links (to other WEB pages or WEB sites)

For maintenance purposes, comments throughout the HTML file may be desirable:

</- - This is a HTML comment   - ->

Example 1:

Type this up in Notepad and save it as Example1.HTML Run it by double-clicking on the file name, whereupon it uses the default browser.

Were the three text lines crammed together? To keep your text formatting, place the relevant text lines between the tags <PRE> and </PRE> Where "PRE" stands for preformatted:

```
<HTML>
<HEAD>
        <TITLE>A Student</TITLE>
</HEAD>

<BODY>
<H1>WELCOME TO DEVRY!</H1><P>
<PRE>I am a CIS student
From Houston
Who wants to program on the Internet!</PRE>
</BODY>
</HTML>
```

To get the font to be size 16 Bold in Times New Roman, utilize the tags <FONT> and </FONT>:

```
<FONT><FONT SIZE = 16 FONT WEIGHT = "bold"
        FONT NAME = "Times New Roman">
</FONT>
```

Modified example:

```
<HTML>
<HEAD>
        <TITLE>A Student</TITLE>
</HEAD>

<BODY>
<H1>WELCOME TO DEVRY!</H1><P>
<FONT><FONT SIZE = 16 FONT WEIGHT = "bold"
        FONT NAME = "Times New Roman">
</FONT>
<PRE>I am a CIS student
From Houston
Who wants to program on the Internet!</PRE>
</BODY>
</HTML>
```

Update Example 1 and save it. Run it from the browser:

Double-click on Internet Explorer to bring up the screen. Click on Open and Browse. Find Example1.HTML to get your page. Then run.

If you have both Internet Explorer and Netscape browsers installed on your computer, one is the default browser. You must get the non-default browser on the screen to run your WEB pages with it.

Sometimes Internet Explorer and Netscape don't show the WEB pages exactly the same. Perhaps you will check on the Server which browser the Caller (user) uses so you can show the WEB page in his browser's format.

Display an image:

> <IMG SRC = "butterfly.gif" WIDTH = 400 HEIGHT = 300
>   ALIGN = CENTER>

SRC stands for source. The file is stored in the same folder as this HTML file. The width and height are in pixels, 8 to a character. The ALIGN default is left.

A link to another HTML page is:

> <A HREF = "SECOND.HTML">GO TO PAGE 2</A>

Only "GO TO PAGE" appears in blue on the screen. SECOND.HTML is stored in the folder as the web page to be linked to. "A" stands for anchor, HREF for HTTP reference.

To link to a WEB site examine:

<A HREF = "http://www.devrylopez.com/yourpage.html">
            GO TO DEVRY</A>

Tables represent headings and data clearly, utilizing the <TABLE>, <TR> (table row), <TH> (table heading> And <TD> (table data).

<H3>EMPLOYEE TABLE</H3>
<TABLE BORDER>
<TR>
    <TH>NAME</TH>
    <TH>JOB</TH>
</TR>

```
<TR>
    <TD>Jones</TD>
    <TD>Programmer</TD>
</TR>

<TR>
    <TD>Smith</TD>
    <TD>Systems Analyst</TD>
</TR>
</TABLE>
```

The word "BORDER" draws lines in the table, but it looks clear without the lines. This example has one heading line, but you could have more. There are two data lines, but you could have more. Indenting facilitates the identification of typing errors

```
<H3>EMPLOYEE TABLE</H3>
<TABLE BORDER>
<TR><TH>NAME</TH><TH>JOB</TH></TR>
<TR><TD>Jones</TD><TD>Programmer</TD></TR>
<TR><TD>Smith</TD><TD>Systems Analyst</TD></TR>
</TABLE>
```

A table can have links:

```
<TR>
    <TD>
            <A HREF = "Smith.html">Smith</A>
            ……………………..
```

Linked lists are an alternative way of representing hierarchical data and WEB links.

An unordered list (ul) uses bullets:

```
<H4>EMPLOYEES</H4>
<UL>
    <LI>Jones</LI>
    <LI>Smith</LI>
</UL>
```

LI stands for line.

The displayed output appears as:

EMPLOYEES
. Jones
. Smith

Display an ordered list (ol) by replacing ul with ol:

```
<H4>EMPLOYEES</H4>
<OL>
      <LI>Jones</LI>
      <LI>Smith</LI>
</OL>
```

LI stands for line. "</LI> is optional.

The displayed output appears as:

EMPLOYEES
1. Jones
2. Smith

Use unordered lists when you don't care what order the list items are in, ordered lists when the order matters!

Insert a link with:

```
<LI>
    <A HREF = "Jones.html">Jones</A>
</LI>
```

Indenting is optional:

```
<LI><A HREF = "Jones.html">Jones</A></LI>
```

A combination of unordered and ordered lists is interesting:

```
<OL>
<LI>Select ingredients</LI>
<UL>
<LI>Cheese</LI>
<LI>Tomato sauce</LI>
<LI>Sausage</LI>
</UL>
<LI>Choose size</LI>
<UL>
<LI>Small</LI>
<LI>Medium</LI>
<LI>Large</LI>
</UL>
</OL>
```

This unordered list within an ordered list displays like this:

1. Select ingredients
    . Cheese
    . Tomato sauce
    . Sausage

2. Choose size
    . Small
    . Medium
    . Large

2.3 Forms

An HTML page utilizes Forms to prompt for, and to accept, data from the computer operator and to initialize actions ("Events"), including the transmittal of this data to the Server Site for processing.

A Form uses <FORM> and </FORM> tags:

```
<HTML>
<HEAD>
<TITLE>Information</TITLE>
</HEAD>
<BODY>

<FORM>

............
</FORM>
</BODY>
</HTML>
```

Display a message with document.writeln:

```
document.writeln("DeVry greets you!");
```

Get data with:

```
Name = Prompt ("Key in your name","Somebody");
```

There are two spaces in a popup box, the first being the request("Key in your name), the second the blue default. If you hit the "Yes" key without keying your name over "Somebody", then that is your name. "Name" now contains your typed-in name, the default name otherwise.

Note that the value of Name is string even if you typed in a number.
Now echo this back to the computer operator:

```
Document.writeln("Welcome to" + Name);
```
As a chunk of instructions:

```
Document.writeln("Welcome to DeVry");
Name = prompt("Key in your name");
Document.writeln("Welcome to" + Name);
```

Suppose you were prompted for a number to be added to a total:

```
Total = prompt("Key in Total Amount", "0");
Amount = Prompt("Key in Amount", "0");
Document.writeln("New total is", parseDouble(Total) + "   " +
                                  parseDouble(Amount));
```

"parseDouble" converts the string to double (i.e., decimal) if it can, to zero otherwise. "Data validation" will be covered in JavaScript scripts in Chapter 3. "parseInt" converts a string to integer.

In Form the "INPUT TYPE" command displays an icon (such as a clickable button), "VALUE" displays a message, and onClick identifies the action to be performed if the button is clicked:

```
<FORM>
<INPUT TYPE = "button" VALUE = "Click for Soup du Jour"
            onClick = 'alert("Oxtail Soup $2.75 a bowl!")'>
</FORM>
```

The button has a visible message of "Click for Soup du Jour!". If it is clicked, an "alert" popup box appears with the message: "Oxtail Soup $2.75 a bowl!". Click on a icon to close the popup box.

This sets up a Form with a label, a textbox, and a button. When the button is clicked it uses the "alert" function to display:

AMOUNT KEYED IS (value of amount)

```
<HTML>
<BODY>
<FORM>
<INPUT TYPE = "label" VALUE = "Key in number">
<INPUT TYPE = "text" NAME = "number">
<INPUT TYPE = "button" VALUE = "Click me!"
        onClick = 'alert("NUMBER IS" + number)'>
</FORM>
</BODY>
</HTML>
```

Key in this HTML file and run it on your Internet explorer browser. Key in 32 and click on the button. What pops up on the screen?

Add
's to right of lines 4, 5, 7. Save and run it. What difference?

The "submit" sends the data to the name indicated in the <FORM> line, which could be an external server site. This will be covered in Chapter 4 (JavaScript).

Clicking the button could branch to a JavaScript function usually within the <HEAD> and </HEAD> tags. This is examined in Chapter 4 ("JavaScript").

More Forms material is covered in Chapter 4 (JavaScript).

2.4 Lab Assignments

2.4.1 Set up a HTML page with:
- heading of your name

body of:
- 3 lines about what type of job you want after
graduation (use PRE)
- a horizontal line
- an image (jpg or gif format, 300 pixels wide and 400 pixels high)

You can search the Internet for suitable images, such as "animal images".
The Author suggests you save the image in the same disk subdirectory where this
HTML WEB page is stored.

2.4.2 Set up an HTML page with:

- heading of Table Demo
- body of:
- a table heading ("Menu")
- one table line: Item & Price
- three data lines (item names & prices)

2.4.3 Add to Lab 3 a link to CREDITCARD.HTML
- create a second page called "CREDITCARD.HTML"
with:
a welcome message to CREDIT CARD PAGE
a link back to your first (and starting page)

2.4.4 Set up an HTML page with:
- Heading of LISTS
- body of:
- list header ("CARS")
- list:
1. Get money
2. Buy car
3. Get gas

2.4.5 Set up a list program with body of:

JOBS (header)
. Programmers
    Java
    Visual BASIC
. Systems Analysts
    Unified Modeling Language
    Agile Methodology

2.4.6 Set up a HTML page with a Form:
- Label (Amount)
- Text (blank, key in amount here)
- Button (onClick converts amount to integer, double it and move its new value to second text button)
- Label (Doubled Amount)
- Text (Will have the doubled amount moved to it by the button's clicked event)

2.4.7 If you have Microsoft's Front Page WEB developer, key in your program and run it. Rather than writing HTML code you will have it generated by the options under the "Insert" menu option.

2.4.8 Set up HTML page :
- Title of "DEVRY GOES TO THE CIRCUS!"
- Body:
    - "GET A GOOD JOB!" (H3 size)
    - image (350 pixels wide & 450 pixels high)
    - Table with border:

NAME	OCCUPATION
Gates	Nerd
Champion	Instructor
Nobody	GoFor

- List: CURRICULA
    . TCOM
        1. Networking
        2. Board Wiring
    . CIS

1. Visual BASIC (+ link to VB.HTML)
2. COBOL (+ link to COBOL.HTML)

- Form: Button ("HUNGRY?"), whose clicking issues an alert of "Any spicy mustard?"

Add VB.HTML and COBOL.HTML, each with a suitable message and a link back to the main (first) HTML page.

2.4.9 Set up an HTML page with:

Get image "giraffe.gif" from same folder this HTML page is stored in, and display it right-aligned 300 pixels wide and 200 pixels deep.

Display an unordered list within an ordered list::

MENU
. MEAT
   Beef
   Ham
   Tofu
. VEGGIE
   Potato
   Peas

2.5 Test Questions

2.5.1 Add a link (to BOB.HTML) to the following TABLE:

```
<TABLE>
<TR>
    <TH>NAME</TH>
    <TH>SALARY</TH>
</TR>

<TR>
    <TD>BOB</TD> // make this a link
    <TD>50000</TD>
</TR>

<TR>
    <TD>MARY</TD>
    <TD>55000</TD>
</TR>
</TABLE>
```

2.5.2 Given: <LI>BOB</LI>

Change the link's reference to the Internet at
www.devrylopez.com/bob.html:

2.5.3 Correct the errors in the following code:

```
…………..
<ul>
    <li>Breakfast</li>
        <ol>
            <li>Cereal</li>
            <li>Milk</li>
    <li>Lunch</li>
        <ol>
            <li>Beef</li>
            <li>Rice</li>
        </ul>
</UL>
………………
```

2.5.4 Write the HTML Body line to call an image HORSE.JPG, sizing it 400 pixels wide and 300 long.

2.5.5 Correct the following table:

```
.............
<table border>
<tr>
      <th>Name</th>
      <th>Car</th>
<tr>
      <td>Bob</td>
      <td>Mercedes</td>
      <td>Joan</td>
      <td>Maserati</td>
</table>
```

2.5.6 Given: <table border>
```
      <tr>
            <td>Jim</td>
            <td>CIS</td>
      </tr>
      </table>
```

Change Jim to link to Jim.html, and CIS to link to www.MySite.com/CIS.asp

---

Chapter 3

Cascading Style Sheets (CSS)

3.0 Objectives

Cascading Style Sheets (CSS) give you more visual and style control over your HTML pages with sophisticated page layout properties.

- Set fonts and colors in your page in a controlled manner

- Set up styles

- Use Contextual selection

3.1 Inline Styles

Given:
```
<HTML>
<HEAD>
        <TITLE>Style</TITLE>
</HEAD>

<BODY>
Welcome to Style
Using Cascading Style Sheets
</BODY>
</HTML>
```

If you want the first line to be green and the second line blue:

```
<P STYLE = "color: Green">Welcome to Style</P>
<P STYLE = "color: Blue">Using Cascading Style Sheets</P>
```

In inline coding each line has its own specific style. Alternatively you May use a hexadecimal color representation:

```
<P STYLE = "color: #008000">Welcome to Style</P>
<P STYLE = "color: #0000FF">Using Cascading Style Sheets</P>
```

Some colors:	Blue	#0000FF	Green	#008000
	Black	#000000	Lime	#00FF00
	Magenta	#FF00FF	Maroon	#800000
	Gray	#808080	Navy	#000080
	Olive	#808000	Cyan	#00FFFF
	Purple	#800080	Teal	#008080
	Red	#FF0000	Yellow	#FFFF00
	Silver	#C0C0C0	White	#FFFFFF

DIV tags set CSS information for specific elements within a Web page, and can be embedded within the Body of an HTML page:

```
<HTML>
<BODY>
<DIV STYLE = "FONT-FAMILY: COURIER; COLOR: RED">
<H1>A red-colored, Courier-font header.</H1>
</DIV>
Back to normal!
</BODY>
</HTML>
```

The LINK tag calls a separate WEB page for the CSS instructions:

```
<HTML>
<HEAD>
<TITLE>Link Example</TITLE>
<LINK REL = STYLESHEET HREF = "formatting.css"
      TYPE = "text/css">
..................................
```

The "formatting.css" file contains only CSS formatting information:

```
<!-- formatting.css comment -->
BODY { FONT-SIZE: X-LARGE; MARGIN: 1 IN}
R {COLOR: RED; BACKGROUND: YELLOW;}
B {COLOR: BLACK;}
```

3.2 Class Styles

To get a style to be applicable to the whole body code the style in HEAD and refer to that style in the body:

```
<HTML>
<HEAD>
<TITLE>More control</TITLE>

<STYLE>B {text = "FONT-TRANSFORM: UPPERCASE"}</STYLE>
</HEAD>

<BODY>
  This displays as usual
<B>But this displays uppercase letters.</B>
</BODY>
</HTML>
```

The style is indented in HEAD as B. Whatever letters are displayed in the BODY between the tags <B> and </B> have uppercase letters.

Another example with colors:

```
<HTML>
<HEAD>
<TITLE>Color control</TITLE>
<STYLE TYPE = "text/css">
     P { color:green; }
     :HeadingRed { color:red; }
</STYLE>
</HEAD>

<BODY>
  This displays as usual
<P>Some green text</P><BR>
<P CLASS = "HeadingRed">True red!</P>
</BODY>
</HTML>
```

To call external CSS pages:

```
<HTML>
<HEAD>
<TITLE>Link example</TITLE>
<LINK REL = STYLESHEET HREF = "formatting.css"
        TYPE = "text/css">
```

The external file (formatting.css) contains only CSS formatting information:

```
<!-- formatting css comment - - >
BODY { FONT-SIZE:X-LARGE; margin: 1 IN;}
R { COLOR:RED; BACKGROUND:YELLOW }
B { COLOR:BLACK }
```

A composite example with ID as Selector:

```
<HTML>
<HEAD>
<TITLE>ID as Selector</TITLE>:
<STYLE>
#GREEN { COLOR:GREEN; FONT-WEIGHT: BOLD; }
</STYLE>
</HEAD>

<BODY>
<H1>A Header</H1>
<P ID = "GREEN">Green text here.</P>

<H2 ID = "GREEN">A green header</H2>

<P>REGULAR HEADER, NOT GREEN, NOT BOLD</P>
</BODY>
</HTML>
```

Internal styles will override styles applied from an external style sheet, giving Cascading Style Sheets their name!

3.3 Contextual Selectors

WEB browsers should be able to apply CSS formatting rules based on the context in which a particular CSS property appears on a WEB page.

The following example has:

  - List lines under an unordered list are extra large black;

In a two-level nested unordered list, the bottom level's lines are large & red.

```
<HTML>
<HEAD>
<STYLE>
    UL LI { FONT-SIZE:X-LARGE; COLOR:BLACK; }
    UL UL LI { FONT-SIZE:LARGE; COLOR = RED; }
</STYLE>

<BODY>
CURRICULA:<BR>
<UL>
        <LI>CIS</LI> /* X-LARGE BLACK */
            <UL>
                <LI>COBOL</LI>         /* LARGE RED */
                <LI>JAVA</LI>          /* LARGE RED */
                <LI>Visual BASIC</LI>  /* LARGE RED */
            </UL>
        <LI>TCOM</LI> /* X-LARGE BLACK */
            <UL>
                <LI>Networks</LI>  /* LARGE RED */
                <LI>C</LI>         /* LARGE RED */
            </UL>
    </UL>
    </BODY>
    </HTML>
```

Buy a book on CSS for further reference. Try some of these techniques in your HTML pages utilizing Microsoft's Internet Explorer (likely to have the latest CSS techniques).

3.4 Lab Assignments

3.4.1 Set up the following HTML page:

- title of "CSS Example"
- body: WELCOME TO STYLE (in H3)

        Courses: (ordered list)
        1. Visual Basic
        2. C#
        3. Java

Now use CSS to:
- make H3 blue
- make the ordered list lines appear in red

3.4.1 Set up an HTML page with:

MAJORS (h3)

. CIS
      1. Systems Analyst
      2. COBOL Programmer

.TI
      1. Telecommunications
      2. C Programmer

- make the h3 heading green

- utilizing Contextual Selection"
      make the unordered list lines red
-    " " ordered list lines blue

3.4.2 Create an HTML page with:
>   Heading Alpha
>   Heading Beta
>   Heading Kappa

Set up a style between the <HEAD> and </HEAD> tags to use A for black size 14, B for red size 12, and K for green size 8.

3.4.3 Test Questions

3.4.5 All CSS styles must exist within the HTML file—True or False?

3.4.6 Write a CSS comment for "Watch my speed!":

3.4.7 If two CSS styles conflict on a coding line, the earlier one prevails—True or False?

Chapter 4

Fundamentals of JavaScript

4.0 Objectives

- utilize JavaScript functions in your HTML pages to:
- read and write data
- validate data
- make the presentation neater
- convert strings to numbers
- do calculations
- make logical comparisons
- perform WHILE and FOR-loops
- load and display arrays

Use Forms in your HTML page to:

- prompt and read in strings

- pass strings to functions
- receive data from functions
- utilize controls (such as buttons) to trigger events

4.1 Introduction

Scripting languages allow HTML WEB pages to handle programming. JavaScript is the standard WEB scripting language, Microsoft's version is JScript (on the .NET platform).

Microsoft made their Active Server Pages (ASP) capable of using JavaScript or VBScript. I utilize JavaScript code because it is a Web standard and runs under .NET.

JavaScript segments are inserted into the HTML code, whether Client-side or Server-side code (examined in 5.3, 5.4, and 5.5, Active Server Pages with JavaScript). A suitable use is to validate data at the Client (local) before submitting the data to the Server Site over The Internet.

If you need VBScript, examine Appendices A and B.

4.2 JavaScript Fundamentals

JavaScript code must be within the <SCRIPT> and </SCRIPT> tags:

```
<HTML>
<BODY>
<H3>Displaying this line.</H3>

<SCRIPT LANGUAGE = "JavaScript"> /* inline coding */
document.writeln("<H2>DeVry greets you!</H2>");
</SCRIPT>
</BODY>
</HTML>
```

An example prompting for input, which is then displayed:

```
<HTML>
<BODY>
<SCRIPT LANGUAGE = "JavaScript"> /* inline coding */
var age = prompt("Key in your age", "39");
document.writeln("Good morning" + age);
</SCRIPT>
</BODY>
</HTML>
```

The age definition has no data type (in JavaScript), so the age is read in as string. To add 1 to the age before displaying it, convert the string age to integer first:

```
var newAge;
newAge = parseInt(age) + 1;
```

Type in this HTML document and run it for confirmation that the arithmetic works: if you key in 21, 22 is displayed! "parseFloat" is used for converting string to decimal fields. Program validation is covered later in this section: Make sure the field is numeric and meets a range of acceptable values before converting it to numeric data type and transmitting it over the Internet!

Often you have a chunk of JavaScript code to be performed upon clicking a button. In this case create a function between the <HEAD> and </HEAD> tags:

```
<HTML>
<HEAD>
        <TITLE>A JavaScript Function</TITLE>
        <SCRIPT LANGUAGE = "JavaScript">
            function displayIt(rent)
            {
                r = parseFloat(rent);
                alert ("Rent =" + r * 1.1); /* 10% rent increase */
            }
        </SCRIPT>
</HEAD>
<BODY>
<FORM>
<INPUT TYPE = "label" VALUE = "KEY IN DECIMAL">
<INPUT TYPE = "text" NAME = "rent">
<INPUT TYPE = "button" VALUE = "CLICK FOR NEW RENT"
            onClick = "displayIt (rent.value)">
</FORM>
</BODY>
</HTML>
```

Line 5 is the start of function displayIt, with the string rent passed to it from the Form after the button is pressed, activating the button's action event.

Line 7 converts rent from string to Float (decimal), so the next line can multiply it by 1.1, representing a 10% rent increase.

Line 8 uses the JavaScript function "alert" for screen display.

Line 14 uses a label to identify what to key into the textbox to its right.

Line 15 is a blank textbox until you key in a number and click the button.

Line 17 sends the string keyed in to the textbox to the JavaScript function "displayIt" when the button is clicked. Pass "rent.value", i.e., the string value of rent. Later, in the ASP page,you may send rent to another site for processing!

Key this in and run it to see how it works, using Internet Explorer.

Validating a number by using the JavaScript function isNaN (amt), being true if string amt is "Not a Number", negative logic!

Validating in the Body:

```
<BODY>
<SCRIPT LANGUAGE = "javascript">
var amt = prompt ("Key in amount", "5.00");
if (isNaN (amt))
{
      document.writeln (amt + "is not a number");
}
else {
            document.writeln (amt + "is numeric");
      }
</SCRIPT>
</BODY>
</HTML>
```

If you also require a valid numeric field to be an integer from 01–20:

```
var amt = prompt ("Key in amount", "5.00");
if (isNaN (amt))
{
      document.writeln (amt + "is not a number");
}
else {
            var amount = parseInt (amt);
            if (amount > = 01 && amount < = 20)
                        /* && means and-logical operation */
            {
                  document.writeln (amt + "is numeric & in range");
            }
      }
                  && means an AND logical operation,!! stands for OR.
```

To do this is more convenient in HEAD in a function, which can be called as the action event of a Form button (which passes the string to the function):

```
<HTML>
<HEAD>
<TITLE>Validating Function"</TITLE>

<SCRIPT LANGUAGE = "JavaScript">
    function validateIt (amt)
    {
        if (isNaN (amt))
          {
              document.writeln (amt + "is not a number");
          }
          else {
                  var amount = parseInt (amt);
                  if (amount > = 01 && amount < = 20)
                          /* && means and-logical operation */
                    {
                        alert ("Taxed Amount is" + amount * 1.08);
                                /* Sales tax is 8%, asterisk is multiplication */
                    }
              }
    }
    </SCRIPT>
    </HEAD>

    <BODY>
    <FORM>
    <INPUT TYPE = "label" VALUE "Key in amount">
    <INPUT TYPE = "text" NAME = "amt">
    <INPUT TYPE = "button" VALUE = "Click for taxed amount"
            onClick = validateIt (amt.value)>
    </FORM>
    </BODY>
    </HTML>
```

4.3 Arithmetic:

The arithmetic operators are:

(a) Basic: + (add), - (subtract), * (multiply, / (division),
        % (modulus, returns the remainder of a division)

- add and subtract have the same priority
- multiply, divide and modulus have the same priority
- set (2) has a higher priority than set (1)

assignment: = (equals),! = (not equal), + = (add by value),
                = (subtract by value), * = (multiply by value),
                / = (divide by value), % = (modulus by value)

Example by value: total + = amt;

- amt is added to total, the result left in total
        (i.e., total both participates in the calculation and is
        where the result is stored)

If you have several items of the same priority in a row, they are computed from left to right:

profit = sales – costs – depreciation;

- first, costs is subtracted from sales; second depreciation is subtracted
-            from that result; final answer is stored in profit.

Example: Average = sales + rent / 2;

To have sales added to rent **before** the divide occurs, utilize a pair of parentheses to override the arithmetic priorities:

Average = (sales + rent) / 2;

4.4 Logical Operators and Comparisons

The logical operators are: = (equal), ! = (not equal),
&& (and), || (or).

Example:

```
if (amt > 70.00)
        alert (amt + "exceeds 70.00");
else alert (amt + "is less than or equal to 70.00");
```

The ELSE action is performed when the if-condition is not true.

Braces { } are required in the actions if two or more actions are performed upon a certain condition being true:

```
if (amt > 70.00)
{
        alert (amt + "exceeds 70.00");
        total + = amt;
}
else {
        alert (amt + "< = 70.00");
        alert ("Cheapscape!");
        }
```

Sometimes multiple conditions must be checked:

&& (and) says that all condition must be true to perform the action:

```
if (money > 100 && numberCars > 0 && marital = "Single")
        alert ("You got the date!");
```

|| (or) says that you get the action performed as long as at least one of the conditions is true:

```
if (age > 20 || money > 25000)
        alert("You may enter the discotec!";
```

"Nested-IF" statements:

```
if (money > 50)
      alert("See Opera")
else if (money > 5)
            alert("See movie")
      else
                  alert("Watch TV");
                  /* default action */
```

If you have many values to check for, consider using a "SWITCH" statement:

```
switch (choice) /* choice is numeric)
{
      case 1:
            alert("ONE");
            break;
      case 2:
            alert("TWO");
            break;
      default:
            alert("Not 1 or 2");
}
```

If choice = 1, display ONE in a popup box. "break" is required to get you out of the SWITCH statement after performing the action; otherwise, after hitting 1, program control would check the remaining conditions also.

4.5 Loops

WHILE-loops continue as long as the condition is true:

```
function addUp()
{
    var amount, total = 0;

    while (total < 100)
    {
        amount = parseInt(prompt("Key in integer amount"));
        total + = amount;
    }

    alert("TOTAL =" + total);
}
```

The FOR-loops do a set number of iterations:

```
function bigTex()
{
    var bigDecimal, Total = 0.00, subscript;

    for (subscript = 0; subscript < 5; subscript++)
    {
        bigDecimal = parseInt(prompt("Key in decimal amount"));
        bigTotal + = bigDecimal;
    }

    alert ("bigTotal =" + bigTotal);
}
```

4.6 Arrays

```
function arrayStuff()
{
      var testArray = new Array();

      testArray[0] = 12;
      testArray[1] = 24;
      testArray[2] = 57;
      ................
```

Alternatives are:

- Intialize array in definition:

```
      var testArray = new Array{12, 24, 57}; // 3 rows
```

- Load it with a FOR-loop:

```
      var subscript;
      var testArray = new Array[3];

      for (subscript = 0; subscript < 3; subscript++)
      {
            testArray[subscript] = parseInt(prompt("Key in integer"));
      }
```

4.7 Strings

Creating a string variable:

    var aStr = "Bill Taylor";

You can concatenate (i.e., combine) several strings into one string:

    var bigString = " Big " + " time " + " on the bayou! ";
                    // Note the blanks to separate the phrases

Alternative:

    var bigString = "Big";

    bigString + = " time ";
    bigString + = "on the bayou!");

Converting an integer to a string:

    var n = new Number(10);

    alert(n.toString());

To find the number of characters in a string:

    var name = "ABCDEFGH";

    alert(getLength(name));

Taking part of a string:

    var name = "BOB JONES";

    lastName = substring(name,4);
    // starting the B at 0, the J of jones is at position 4
    // and continuing through the end of the string

4.8 Processing Form Data

4.8.1 Radio Buttons

```
<HTML>
<HEAD>
<SCRIPT LANGUAGE = "javascript">
 var tot1 = 0, tot2 = 0, tot3 = 0;

    function totrtn (same)
    {
        if (same.value == 1)
           tot1 = tot1 + 1;
        else if (same.value == 2)
                tot2 = tot2 + 1;
            else
                    tot3 = tot3 + 1;
    }

    function displayTot()
    {
        alert(" Total beef is " + tot1 + " Total veggie is " +
                tot2 + " Total soup is " + tot3);
    }
<.SCRIPT>
</HEAD>

<BODY>
<FORM>
Beef? <INPUT TYPE = "radio" name = "same" value = "1"
        onClick = "totrtn(this)"><p>
Veggie? <INPUT TYPE = "radio" name = "same" value = "2"
        onClick = "totrtn(this)"><p>
Soup? <INPUT TYPE = "radio" name = "same" value = "3"
        onClick = "totrtn(this)"><p>
Totals? <INPUT TYPE = "button" name = "Totals" value = "Totals"
        onClick = "displayTot()">
</FORM>
</BODY>
</HTML>
```

The JavaScript's "var" definitions are global to all the following functions (totrtn and displayTot).

The radio buttons are grouped together with the same name ("same"). When a particular button is pressed, its value is passed to function totrtn with:

onClick = "totrtn(this)">

In the function, the value passed (same) is checked for its value (same.value) in a programmer's solution

4.8.2 List Options

```
<HTML>
<HEAD>
<SCRIPT LANGUAGE = "javascript">
 var tot1 = 0, tot2 = 0, tot3 = 0;

function totrtn(same)
{
     if (same.value == 1)
        tot1 = tot1 + 1;
     else if (same.value == 2)
            tot2 = tot2 + 2;
          else
              tot3 = tot3 + 1;
}

function displayTot()
{
     alert(" Total beef is " + tot1 + " Total veggie is " +
           tot2 + " Total soup is " + tot3);
}

</SCRIPT>
</HEAD>

<BODY>
<FORM>
Beef? <INPUT TYPE = "radio" name = "same" value = "1"
        onClick = "totrtn(this)"><P>
Veggie? <INPUT TYPE = "radio" name = "same" value = "2"
        onClick = "totrtn(this)"><P>
Soup? <INPUT TYPE = "radio" name = "same" value = "3"
        onClick = "totrtn(this)"><P>

Totals? <INPUT TYPE = "button' name = "Totals" value = "Totals"
        onClick = "displayTot()">
</FORM>
</BODY>
</HTML>
```

The radio buttons are grouped together by the common name of "same".

When a radio button is clicked on, function totrtn is called,
passing the value of that radio button:

```
onClick = "totrtn(this)">
```

The function uses "same.value" to check the actual value passed.
By placing the JavaScript variables (tot1, tot2, tot3) just after the
<SCRIPT LANGUAGE = JavaScript>, these variable are global to the functions.

The totals are started with zero, but are added to separately during each call
of function totrtn.

4.9 Lab Assignments

4.9.1 Create an HTML page with:

Title of MyValidation
Body with:
- JavaScript function "hungry"
- activated by clicking form button hungry
- action is to display: "WHERE'S THE BEEF?"

- JavaScript function validate: activated by clicking form button Validate
  action: if not numeric issue error message

> if numeric:
> - convert string to integer
> - if integer not in range 30-79
>   issue error message
> - if in range double & display result

Form:
- button hungry named hungry, if clicked activate
  function hungry
- textbox named DATAIN
- button named Validate, if clicked activate
  function validate

4.9.2 Create an HTML page with a Form and a JavaScript function within the <HEAD> and </HEAD> tags.

In JavaScript:

Create variables for Income, Costs and Profit.

Function checkIncome: receives Income string; convert it to integer and check for exceeding 500; if not acceptable, move zero to numeric value & issue suitable error message.

Function checkCosts: receives Costs string; convert it to integer and check for exceeding 500; if not acceptable, move zero to numeric value & issue suitable error message.

Function rtnCompute: compute Profit by subtracting the numeric value of Costs from Income and displaying:

PROFIT IS (value of Profit)

Form: textboxes for Income and Costs with label identifiers
button whose clicking calls function rtnCompute,
passing the values of Income and Costs.

4.9.3 Alter lab 4.9.2 to use a Form in the Body instead of the script in the body:
- textbox: amt
- button—if clicked, do function Triple, passing the textbox value

4.9.4 In HTML body use JavaScript to setup a five-row integer array and sub-script, total, string, and average variables. Prompt and read integer values, converting each to integer and:
- Inserting the integer value into the array
- adding the integer value to the total

After the loop is completed, compute and display the decimal average.

4.10 Test Questions

4.10.1 Given strings: var name = "JOHNSMITH";
               var first, last;

   In Server JavaScript code:

   - use substring to move the first four characters of name to first
   - "   "   "   "   " last five characters of name to last
   - use "document.writeln" to display:

                 FIRST NAME = (value of first)
                 LAST NAME = (value of last)

4.10.2 In JavaScript code a "select case" for a multiway branch based on the prompted integer value of "detour":

                 var detour = prompt ("Key integer from 0 to 4", "0");

4.10.3 Given: <BODY>
                 <SCRIPT LANGUAGE = "JavaScript">
                 var customers = new customers();
                 var total = 0, subscript;

   Using a FOR-loop:
      - prompt & read customer #
      - convert string to integer
      - insert integer into the array
      - add the integer to total

   After loop is completed, compute the decimal average & display:

                 AVERAGE = (value of average)

4.10.4 Given: <HTML>
                <HEAD>
                <TITLE>My Quiz"</TITLE>

    (set up JavaScript function Triple, receiving amt from Body,
        convert amt to integer, triple and display new value
        with an alert)

```
</HEAD>
<BODY>
<SCRIPT LANGUAGE = "JavaScript">
var amt;

amt = prompt ("Key in integer amount", "5.00");
triple (amt.value);
</SCRIPT>
</BODY>
</HTML>
```

4.10.5 Correct the following JavaScript code for logical errors:

```
function total (amt)
{
    if (isNaN (amt))
        alert (parseInt (amt));
    else
        alert ("Non-numeric");
}
```

Chapter 5

Active Server Pages with Active Data Objects

5.0 Objectives

- utilize scripting Server-side code in JavaScript

- use a Form button to go from a Client computer to a Server with data

- have a Server receive data, convert to numbers and do arithmetic

- display data in an HTML table

- do data validation on the server

- utilize a database on the Server utilizing Active Data Objects with SQL commands

5.1 Introduction to ASP

Using the Internet involves commands and data passing back-and-forth between Clients and Web Sites. Active Server Pages (ASP) is Microsoft's Open Architecture for this, running client-side coding on the Client's computer and Server-Side coding on the WEB Server.

ASP works with both JavaScript and VBScript. ASP is popular because you can run Server software from your local Client computer. Perhaps Microsoft will rent you their Office Suite on the Internet!

Microsoft JScript runs JavaScript coding, and comes with Microsoft .NET. With ASP the text uses JavaScript examples

>   <SCRIPT LANGUAGE = JavaScript> and </SCRIPT>

With ASP.NET JScript is the default scripting language:

>   <SCRIPT> and </SCRIPT>

5.2 Client-Side Coding Calling the Server

In your HTML file:

(1) Add an action to the FORM telling the computer where to go on the Internet (i.e., to a particular WEB Server) when the form's SUBMIT is clicked, and which type of server (GET or POST) is wanted.

In the following example all the input boxes' contents are made available to the server once the SUBMIT button is clicked:

```
<HTML>
<HEAD>
<TITLE>Client-Server Communication</TITLE>

</HEAD>

<BODY>
Please provide the following information:
<FORM NAME = "MyForm"
    ACTION = "http://www.yoursite.com/yourLab.asp"
           METHOD = "POST">
Price: <INPUT TYPE = "text" NAME = "Price"><br>
Mailin:<INPUT TYPE = "text" NAME = "Mailin"><p>
<INPUT TYPE = "submit" VALUE = "SUBMIT"
            NAME = "Compute Charge">
</FORM>
</BODY>
</HTML>
```

The data type here may as well be "text" as "long" since the data is made available to the Server as strings. To use Price and Mailin on the Server in computations, convert them to a numeric format.

Where do you perform data validation, on the Client before data transmission, or on the Server after transmission? Client-side validation lets the User correct his data before transmission, having the most knowledgeable person correct the data and saving back-and-forth validation questions between the Client and the Server!

"GET" appends all the form data submitted to the URL in the queryString, which the server-side script reads by using Request.QueryString.

"POST" (recommended) submits the form data in the body of the HTML POST command, with the Server reading the data with Request.Form.

You can type the code into NotePad, or utilize a HTML editor (such as HomeSite) or a WEB Developer (such as Microsoft's FrontPage). The HTML file must be saved as text with the suffix "HTML". The file should run under both Microsoft's Internet Explorer or Netscape's Navigator. There may be visual differences in the HTML file appearance between the two browsers.

5.3 Server Execution of ASP Code

This file must be text saved with the suffix ".asp". ASP files run on the Server, in our case after being prompted by the SUBMIT button from the Client. The file must identify the scripting language as the first line of code, or assume the default (JScript on Internet Explorer, JavaScript on Netscape).

The ASP file must be sent to the Server before being used, perhaps by FTP (file transfer protocol):

- go to DOS prompt and type ftp (followed by pressing the Enter key)
- type: open (followed by pressing Enter)
- type: ftp.yoursite.com (and Enter)
- type in your site name & password
- type: send (and Enter)
- type: cd /www (and Enter)
- type source: a:/yourLab.asp (and Enter)
- type destination name: yourLab.asp (and Enter)
- check CRT-screen for confirmation

Repeat this process if you change the file at a:\yourLab.asp. Often industry users have a FTP package (such as CuteFtp) to expedite this process. The Author uses AOL ftp (Click on keyword, type in ftp, Enter, click on other sites and follow the screen prompting).

For testing purposes you could utilize Microsoft's Personal WEB Server (PWS) or Information Server IIs (version 5) as "localhost". Save the ASP file at c:\inetpub\wwwroot, assuming you have the WEB administrator's script permission to save and run scripts.

Code to be run only on the Server (server-side code)is enclosed between the <% and %> tags.

Examine the following ASP code matching the Client-side HTML file in the previous section:

```
<% @LANGUAGE = "javascript" %>
<HTML>
<TITLE>At the Server!</TITLE>
<BODY>
The Server has retrieved the form data:<p>
<% var p, m;
      p = Request.Form("Price");
      m = Request.Form("Mailin");
%>

Price:      <% = p %><br>
Mailin:    <% = m %><p>
Total:      <% = parseInt(p) + parseInt(m) %>
</BODY>
</HTML>
```

Request.Form("Price") requests the Price string from the Client. Variables with no data types hold this data at the Server until the run is completed.

The tags <% and %> contain JavaScript code. The tags <% = and %> contain a data item, perhaps after data conversion ("parseInt") and calculations. The HTML page appears on the Client's CRT-screen after the Server-Side processing.

Could you combine both the client HTML file and the server ASP file? Yes, but only in one ASP file residing on the Server. With our setup you call the HTML file locally on your browser, and it, in turn, calls the ASP file on the WEB Server. You can do all this with a WEB development system such as Front Page, "publishing" the ASP file to the Server.

5.4 Table Display of Data

Utilizing HTML's table tag results in a neater display:

```
<% @LANGUAGE = "javascript" %>
<HTML>
<TITLE>At the Server!</TITLE>
<BODY>
The Server has retrieved the form data:<p>
<% var p, m;
    p = Request.Form("Price");
    m = Request.Form("Mailin");
%>

<TABLE BORDER>
<TR>
    <TH>Price</TH>
    <TH>Mailin</TH>
    <TH>Total</TH>
</TR>

<TR>
    <TD><% = p %></TD>
    <TD><% = m %></TD>
    <TD><% = parseInt(P) + parse.Int(M) %></TD>
</TR>
</TABLE>
</BODY>
</HTML>
```

5.5 Data Validation

In JavaScript the "isNaN" function (i.e., is not numeric) is utilized to check a string for being non-numeric:

```
<HTML>
<TITLE>HTML with JavaScript</TITLE>
<BODY>
<SCRIPT LANGUAGE = "JavaScript">
  var c, t;
  function Validate (costs, taxes)
  {
     if(isNaN(costs)) // true if not numeric
     {
          document.writeln("costs not numeric; please rekey");
          c = 0; // In case the User ignores the error message
     }
     else {
          c = parseInt(costs);
          if!(c > = 0 && c < = 100) // Check numeric range
          {
            document.writeln("costs not in range; please rekey");
            c = 0;
          }
        }

     if(isNaN(taxes)) // true if not numeric
     {
       document.writeln("taxes not numeric; please rekey");
       c = 0; // In case the User ignores the error message
     }
     else {
          t = parseInt(taxes);
          if!(t > = 0 && t < = 100) // Check numeric range
          {
          document.writeln("tax not in range; please rekey");
          t = 0;
          }
     }
  }
```

```
</SCRIPT>
<FORM NAME = "MyForm"
    ACTION = "http://www.yoursite.com/yourLab.asp"
    METHOD = "POST">
COSTS: <INPUT TYPE = "text" VALUE = "costs"><br>
TAXES: <INPUT TYPE = "text" VALUE = "taxes"><p>
<INPUT TYPE = "button" NAME = "Validate" VALUE = "Validate"
    onClick = "Validate_onClick(costs.value, taxes.value)"><p>
<INPUT TYPE = "submit" NAME = "submit" NAME = "Compute Charge">
</FORM>
</BODY>
</HTML>
```

This HTML file runs on the Client computer, so errors can be corrected locally before the data is transmitted to the ASP file (yourName.asp) on the Server. Clicking the first button goes to function "validate" to validate the form fields (costs.value and taxes.value).

If each value is numeric, the validation also includes a range check. If any test is failed, the User is invited to rekey the number and revalidate it. Just in case the User ignores the error message, the numeric value is set to zero, avoiding numeric failures if the Server tries to do an addition involving the two transmitted values.

The ASP file on the Server is not changed when you add validation to the Client HTML file.

5.6 Active Data Objects

5.6.1 ADO

Active Data Objects is Microsoft's latest data access software: ADO first, then ADO.NET running under ASP.NET (examined in the next chapter). The dataset must be saved on the Server and used as OLEDB for Access databases and other Windows databases.

Given an Access database named newdeal.mdb with table named Table1 stored in c:\temp, **register it in ODBC** (Object Database Connectivity) running on XP Professional:

- press start
- select Control Panel
- click on Administrative Tools
- choose DSN and click OK
- select Microsoft access driver
- click Finish
- click on "Select Directory" for all files
- find your database and click on its name
- type in your database name (such as newdeal)
- key in a concise description of your database
- click on OK

- An example (database.asp):

```
<% @LANGUAGE = "javascript" %>
<%
    var objConn, objRS, strQ, strConnection;

    objConn = Server.CreateObject("ADODB.Connection");
    strConnection = "DSN = newdeal; Database = newdeal; UID = sa; PSW = ";
    objConn.Open(strConnection);
    objRS = Server.CreateObject("ADODB.RecordSet");
    objRS.ActiveConnection = objConn;
    strQ = "Select * from Table1";
    objRS = objConn.Execute(strQ);
%>
<HTML>
<BODY>
<%    while(objRS.EOF == false)
    {
        Response.Write(objRS("part") + " ");
        Response.Write(objRS("price") + " ");
        objRS.MoveNext();
    }
    objRS.close();
    objConn.close();
%>
</BODY>
</HTML>
```

The visual output is improved by utilizing a Table within the HTML:

```
    <BODY>
    <TABLE BORDER>
    <TR>
        <TH>PART</TH>
        <TH>PRICE</TH>
    </TR>
    <%
        while(objRS.EOF == false)
        {
            %>
```

```
        <TR>
            <TD><% = Response.Write(objRS("part").value) %></TD>
            <TD><% = Response.Write(objRS("price").value) %></TD>
        </TR>

        <%    objRS.MoveNext();
    }

    objRS.close();
    objConn.close();
%>
```

5.7 Lab Assignments

5.7.1 Set up an HTML page with a form containing text boxes (Income, Costs, Depreciation) and a submit button to your site (and labAsp.asp):

www.yoursite.com/labAsp.asp

Set up your asp page (labAsp.asp) to be stored on your server: retrieve the passed data fields with Request.QueryString. Display this data on the screen, convert the three passed fields to integer, compute Profit by subtracting the numeric Costs and depreciation from Income, and display the Profit.

You need to FTP (file transfer) to my site ftp.yoursite.com with your site name & password when prompted.

Run the HTML file on your computer (the Client, 127.0.0.1 or localhost) and it will transfer control to the ASP file when you click on then Form's submit Button (using the "POST" method).

5.7.2 Run on your local server, perhaps Microsoft's Personal Web server (pws) or IIS (version 5 running under Windows NT2000 or XP Professional).

Create an Access data base Business with table Inventory:
- Part number (99, key)
- Part name (15 characters maximum)
- Price (currency)

Add in five records (2 with prices < = 250, 3 with prices exceeding 250), save it and register the database in ODBC under the Business name.

Create an ASP file (BigData.asp) that:

- Makes a connection to your ODBC-registered database
- Create and execute the SQL command that places in
-     The RecordSet records with prices exceeding 250.
- Start a Table with a heading
- Utilize a WHILE-loop to read and display the table
-     Row values in the table
- Save this ASP file on your local computer in:

C:\inetpub\wwwroot

- Call the ASP file from Internet Explorer:

http://127.0.0.1/BigData.asp

5.7.3 Create an Access database with table Item: fields are part # (key, 999), part-name (15 characters maximum), price (9999v99). Insert 6 records, with prices exceeding 250.00, 3 with prices < = 250.00

Register the file in ODBC on the Server you intend to run ASP on. Create an HTML file with a form submit button to call your ASP file Locally: http://127.0.0.1/MyLab.asp

Create an ASP file that: (1) makes a connection to your ODBC-registered database; (2) create & execute the SQL command that places in the RecordSet records whose prices exceed 250.00; (3) start a Table with a heading line; (4) use a WHILE-loop to read & display each record (row) of the database table; (5) save this ASP file in: c:\inetput\wwwroot; (6) Call the HTML file from Internet Explorer & click the button.

Create a client HTML page with: (1) in Form use input textboxes to get Income & costs, a submit button to transmit the data (income & sales) to the Server ASP page.

Create an ASP page with: (1) Set up variable for income & sales (but with different names) & netIncome; (2) use Request.Form to load the data (income & costs); (3) display the data; (4) convert the data to float and compute netIncome by subtracting costs (numeric) from income (numeric); (5) display netIncome.

5.8 Test Questions

5.8.1 Code the SQL command to delete the record with id of "TEXAS" from database Orion, table COMET:

5.8.2 Code the SQL command to insert a new record into database ORION, Table COMET:

> part = 72
> name = "Rivet"
> qty = 10000
> price = 0.04

5.8.1 How is "localhost" related to "127.0.0.1"?

5.8.2 The "GET" method in a Form displays the transmitted data to the Server in the HTTP header to the right with ampersands. T or F?

5.8.3 To send your ASP program to the external Server over the Internet with Email. T or F?

5.8.4 Complete the following JavaScript loop on the Server to control reading the disk file:

> While (objRS.EOF _____)
> ....

5.8.5 Correct the following Server-side JavaScript to run correctly:

```
<%  var A = objRS("qty");
    var B = objRS("price");
    var C = A * B;

    response.write(A + " " + B + " " + C);
%>
```

5.8.6 After completing reading a database file on the Server, why do the following:

> objRS.close( );
> objConn.close( );

_____

Why is it better to validate data at the Client than at the Server?

_____

Chapter 6

ASP.NET and ADO.NET

6.0 Objectives

- Read and update an ASP.NET file with SQL commands.
- Utilize ASP.NET files with JScript, C# and VB.NET scripting.

6.1 Introduction to ASP.NET

The .NET version of ASP is ASP.NET, although you can still run ASP under
.NET. ADO.NET requires the use of a .NET-compatible WEB Server, such as
Microsoft Internet Information Server IIs. The ADO.NET file is compiled on
the Server before running.

File names require the suffix ".aspx". Information Server (IIS) 5.0 processes this file type through a special Internet Server Application Program Interface (ISAPI) filter that handles the requested WEB form.

The Microsoft .NET implementation of ASP.NET is WebForms, which consists of two files:

(1) One file holds the HTML and is saved with the suffix "aspx";

(2) The other file contains the user services code in the "code-behind" page (whose suffix is "aspx.cs" for C#, or "aspx.vb" for VB.NET).

Why move from ASP to ASP.NET?

- utilize C# and VB.NET as scripting languages in WebForms because compiled code runs faster

- availability of WebForms (which are compiled before use)

- full support of XML, CSS (Cascading Style Sheets) and other WEB standards

- access to the .NET platform, extending the Windows API

- built-in security from the Windows Server

- integrates with ADO.NET for database access

6.2 ASP.NET Visually

It is easy to build a form visually. When you start an ASP.NET application an application is created on the Server.

(1) Click on File, New, Project, C# Application, ASP.NET Application and OK;

(2) Select View and ToolBox;

(3) Click on TextBox and move it to the form, resizing as desired;

(4) Click on f4 (Properties) and change Text's contents to "WATCH ME!" and click the Enter key;

(5) Click on ToolBox and button, and move the button to the form, resizing as desired;

(6) Click f4 and change the button's Text Property to "CLICK ME!";

(7) Double-click the button to get to the place in the code where you key in the following event code (to be done when the button is clicked):
TextBox1.Text = "CONTACT MADE!";

(8) Save, build and run the Project.

To utilize HTML code instead of the Form, when the Form first appears, click HTML at the bottom of the Form. "Visual Form Creation" automatically builds the code for you, where you can change code, or insert code.

6.3 Scripting Languages for ASP.NET

You can utilize:

(1) JScript (runs JavaScript code);

(2) C#;

(3) VB.NET (Visual Basic.NET).

Like Java (with Java Server Pages), ASP.NET uses a full programming language if you like: either C# or VB.NET. Since both C# and VB.NET are compiled to ILS (intermediate language), VB.NET is likely to be popular because of ease of use.

Microsoft's proprietary scripting language VBScript is covered in Appendices A and B, but it doesn't work under the .NET platform.

The ASP.NET files are saved with the suffix ".aspx". Such files are run only on the server (which must be ASP.NET capable, running the Windows NT 4.0, 2000 or XP Professional operating systems). The Author runs locally with the Microsoft Internet Information Server (IIs, version 5 or 6).

6.3.1 JScript

The simplest way to run this:

Step 1: Start Visual Studio.net, selecting File, New, Project, C#, type in project name, OK, HTML (choice at left-bottom of form)

Step 2: Insert just before "</head>":

```
<script language = "jscript">
function addBill(bill)
{
  var pay;

  pay = parseFloat(bill) * 1.05;
  alert("Pay total bill of" + pay);
}
</script>
```

Step 3: Insert just before "</form>":

```
Key in bill: <input type = "text" name = "bill"><br><br>
<input type = "button" value = "Compute total"
    name = "compute" onClick = "addTax(bill.value)">
```

Save, build and run (without debugging).

6.3.2 C#

In Sun's "Java Server Pages" (JSP), the computer language Java is your scripting language:

Advantages: - you get a full compilation with useful error messages, expediting error correction.

- compiled code runs faster.

Disadvantage - you must know the Java programming language

Microsoft allows you to utilize C# (or VB.NET) as your scripting language with similar advantages (and disadvantages).

Example:

- Choose File, New, Project, C# Applications, and ASP.NET Web Applications

- Type in your project name.

- Wait until your new web application is ready (utilizing, perhaps, Microsoft's IIs (5) Information Server).

- Add to the form:

A textbox for sales
A button
A textbox for newSales

- Double-click on an empty space of the form to get to
-     the code (C#) for WebForm1.aspx.cs.

- Type the following code in the method
-     Button1_Click (object sender, System.EventArgs e):

```
double s = Double.Parse(TextBox1.Text) * 1.25;
TextBox2.Text = s;
```

- Save all, build and run (without debugging).

You have special functions available for validation. The following would be added to the "code-behind" page for C#:

(a) Add inside the <HEAD> and </Head> TAGS:

```
<script language = "C#" runat = "server">
    void Button1_Click (Object sender, EventArgs e)
    {
        rangeValInteger.Validate();
        if (rangeValInteger.IsValid)
        {
                txtBox1.Text = "Result: Valid";
        }       // an ELSE does not work here;
    }           // use ErrorMessage in the RangeValidator to issue
</script>       // an out-of-range message
```

(b) Add the following code between the <BODY> and </BODY> tags:

```
<form runat = "server">
<asp:button id = "Button1" text = "Validate"
     onClick = "Button1_Click" runat = "server" />
<asp:TextBox id = "txtBox1" runat = "server" />

<asp:RangeValidator id = "rangeValInteger" type = "integer"
        ControlToValidate = "txtBox1"
        MaximumValue = "10" MinimumValue = "01"
        ErrorMessage = "Not in range 01-10" runat = "server" />
</form>
```

NOTES:

- The "RangeValidator" includes the low and high range values when the button is clicked, the script function in HEAD issues a success message if the value in "txtBox1" is in the range 01-10

- The "ErrorMessage" option in the FORM is performed if the value in "txtBox1" is not in range (01-10).

If you want an error message for not entering three alphabetic characters (upper or lower-case) into textbox name, insert the following code into the Body

```
<asp:RegularValidationExpression id = "name" type = "text"
     ControlToValidate = "name"
     ErrorMessage = "Not 3 alphabetic characters"
     RegularValidationExpression = "[a-zA-Z] {3} runat = "server" />
```

Notes: [a-zA-Z] accepts only alphabetic characters

        {3} allows only three characters to be entered

6.3.3 VB.NET

Visual Basic.NET can also be utilized as your scripting language, with full compilation, giving useful error messages on syntax errors.

Example:

- Choose File, New, Project, Visual Basic Applications,
-      and ASP.NET Web Applications

- Type in your project name.

- Wait until your new web application is ready (utilizing, perhaps, Microsoft's IIs 5 Information Server).

- Add to the form:

A textbox for sales
A button
A textbox for newSales

- Double-click on the form's button form to get to
-      the code (VB.NET) for WebForm1.aspx.vb.

- Type the following code in the subroutine

```
Private Sub Button1_Click(ByVal sender as System.Object,
    ByVal e as System.EventArgs) Handles Button1_Click

    Dim s as Double;
    S = CDbl(TextBox1.Text)* 1.25; // Convert to double
    TextBox2.Text = s;
    End Sub
```
- Save all, build and run (without debugging).

You can also access a database. See previous section for a C# example.

6.4 ADO.NET

ADO.NET is the latest version of Microsoft's "Active Data Objects", designed to communicate with Microsoft's "Component Object Model" (COM) framework under .NET architecture.

Why switch from ADO to ADO.NET?

- ADO.NET is the latest version of Microsoft's "Active Data Objects" designed to communicate with Microsoft's

- "Component object Model (COM)" framework under .NET architecture

- Microsoft's SQL Server 2000 database works easily and efficiently with ADO.NET

6.4.1 ADO.NET with OLEDB

Example of using ADO.NET with an Access database within a C# Windows Application with OLEDB (with SQL Server as an alternative):

- Select Project, New, C#, Windows Application
- Type in project name and "next"
- In the Form move a Grid Box to the form and rename it "lbProducts"
- Double-click in the form to open the Form1_Load event handler
- At the top of the page insert:

      Using System.Data.OleDb;

- Return to the event handler (after the next two lines):

```
private void Form1_Load(object sender, System.EventArgs e)
{
      string strConnection = "provider = Microsoft.JET.OLEDB.4.0;" +
          "data source = c:\\temp\\stuff.mdb";

      string strCommand = "Select * from Table1";

      OleDbDataAdapter dataAdapter =
          new OleDbDataAdapter(strCommand, strConnection);

      DataSet dataSet = new DataSet();

      dataAdapter.Fill(dataSet, "Table1");

      productDataGrid.DataSource =
          dataSet.Tables["Table1"].DefaultView;
   }
 }
}
```

Assuming you have created an Access database stuff.mdb (table is Table1 with part, name and price fields) in c:\temp with data in it, compile and run!

The following program was run using C#.NET on XP Professional, illustrates reading/displaying the contents of a Microsoft Access database utilizing OLEDB:

```csharp
using System;
namespace WindowsApplication1
{
    using System;
    using System.Collections;
    using System.ComponentModel;
    using System.Data;
    using System.Data.OleDb;

    class Class1
    {
        static void Main(string[] args)
        {
            string source = "Provider = Microsoft.Jet.OLEDB.4.0;" +
                "data source = c:\\temp\\db3.mdb";

            string select = "Select * from Students";

            OleDbConnection conn = new OleDbConnection(source);

            conn.Open();

            OleDbCommand cmd = new OleDbCommand(select, conn);

            OleDbDataReader aReader = cmd.ExecuteReader();

            while(aReader.Read())
                {
                Console.WriteLine("{0} {1}",
                    aReader.GetInt32(0), aReader.GetString(1));
                }

            aReader.Close();
            conn.Close();
        }
    }
}
```

Alternatives in utilizing a DataSet:

Improvements are:

(1) Display headings and data in a HTML Table;

(2) Be able to add, change and delete records.

The following OLEDB code is in two phases:

- First, the dataset has a record deleted "Delete from Table1 where part = 40". This marks the record as deleted, but doesn't actually update it.

  Second, the **dataAdapter.Fill(dataSet, "Table1");** code updates the Access 2002 database.

  Third, the database is read ("Select * from Table1); and displayed on the CRT-screen in a grid box.

```
private void Form1_Load(object sender, System.EventArgs e)
{
        string strConnection = "provider = Microsoft.JET.OLEDB.4.0;" +
                        "data source = c:\\temp\\stuff.mdb";

        string strCommand = "Delete from Table1 where part = 40"; // First

        OleDbDataAdapter dataAdapter = new OleDbDataAdapter(
                    strCommand, strConnection);
        DataSet dataSet = new DataSet();
        dataAdapter.Fill(dataSet, "Table1"); // Second

        strCommand = "Select * from Table1"; // Third
        OleDbDataAdapter dataAdapter2 = new OleDbDataAdapter(
                strCommand, strConnection);
        DataSet dataSet2 = new DataSet();
        dataAdapter2.Fill(dataSet2, "Table1");
        productDataGrid.DataSource =
                    dataSet2.Tables["Table1"].DefaultView;
}
```

In phase First, **insert a record** with:
Insert into Table1 values (35, "delta", 45.78);

Add, delete and change selected records with:

-   Select part, price from Table1

-   Select * from Table1 where price > 10.00

-   Delete from Table1 where part = 27

-   Insert into Table1 (part, name, price)
-       VALUES (10,"table",78.89)

-   Select * from Table1 order by price DESC

-   Select * from Authors INNER JOIN books
-       on Authors.ID = books.ID

The following OLEDB example:
-   Deletes a record with no error messages.
-   Inserts a new record with an error message if invalid insert because that record already exists. Inside a TRY/CATCH block the actual insert command
    **OleDbAdapter dataAdapter3 = new OleDbAdapter(
        OleDbCommand, oleDbConnection1);**
    raises an OleDbException if an invalid insert occurs.

```
private void Form1_Load(object sender, System.EventArgs e)
{
        string oleDbConnection1 = "provider = Microsoft.JET.OLEDB.4.0;" +
                            "data source = c:\\temp\\stuff.mdb";

        string oleDbCommand = "Delete from Table1 where part = 85";
        OleDbDataAdapter dataAdapter = new OleDbDataAdapter(
            oleDbCommand, oleDbConnection1);
        DataSet dataSet = new DataSet();
        dataAdapter.Fill(dataSet, "Table1");
```

```
try
{
    oleDbCommand = "Insert into Table1 (part,name,price) values
        (100,'centro',78.78)";
    OleDbDataAdapter dataAdapter3 = new OleDbDataAdapter(
            oleDbCommand, oleDbConnection1);
    DataSet dataSet3 = new DataSet();
    dataAdapter3.Fill(dataSet3, "Table1");

    oleDbCommand = "Select * from Table1";
    OleDbDataAdapter dataAdapter2 = new OleDbDataAdapter(
            oleDbCommand, oleDbConnection1);
    DataSet dataSet2 = new DataSet();
    dataAdapter2.Fill(dataSet2, "Table1");
    productDataGrid.DataSource =
        dataSet2.Tables["Table1"].DefaultView;
}

catch (OleDbException ex)
{ textBox1.Text = "Invalid Insert"; }
}
}
```

6.4.2 Microsoft Data Engine (MSDE)

An alternative uses the MSDE (Microsoft Database Engine) which comes with C#, VB.NET and Visual Studio.NET). The MSDE is a small version of SQL Server. SQL Server works especially easily with .NET. Your maximum dataset size is 2 gigabytes.

To install the MSDE:

- choose start
- click Microsoft.NET Framework SDK
- select Programs
- install the "Install the .NET Frameworks Samples Database"
- install "Set Up the QuickStarts"
- check to see if MSDE is running with
  - Start
  - Control Panel
  - Administrative Tools/Services
  - MSSQL$NetSDK is MSDE
- Close this window
- Go into Visual Studio
- Server Explorer
- Right-click on Data Connections (or "Create New SQL Server Database")
- Choose Add Connection
- Select server name: MSSQL$NetSDK
- Click on "Use Windows NT integrated security"
- Select the database on the Web, such as: Northwind

- create IIs virtual directory (such as localhost/quickstart/aspplus)
- start the ASP.NET QuickStart Tutorial

Or you can purchase a full copy of Microsoft's SQL Server 2000 Developer, $500 as the least expensive version of SQL Server!

You can use the MSDE (Microsoft Database Engine), which is on your .NET installation CD-ROMs. It is a limited (to 2 gigabytes) version of Microsoft SQL Server database. Such a database would be easy to upgrade to a regular SQL Server database.

You can read the tables from Microsoft's "Northwind" database project utilizing the same instructions utilized in SQL Server (SQL, instead of OLEDB).

The following example uses MSDE, C# as the scripting language, and the Northwind database with table customers:

(1) Add a DataGrid control(Dgd) to the form;

(2) Double-click on the form to get to the Page_Load event handler;

(3) Enter code inside the Page_Load's brackets {}:

```
SqlConnection cn = new SqlConnection("server = (local)\\NetSDK;" +
    "uid = sa;pwd = ;database = Northwind;integrated security = true");
                // add in "\\NetSDK if using MSDE

SqlDataAdapter da = new SqlDataAdapter("Select * from customers",
    cn);

DataSet ds = new DataSet();
da.Fill(ds, "customers"); // load dataGrid with table records

Dgd.DataSource = ds.Tables["customers"].DefaultView;
Dgd.DataBind();
```

(4) Add with the other usings: using System.Data.SqlClient;

A revision to utilize a "foreach" loop:

```
SqlConnection cn = new SqlConnection("server = (local)\\NetSDK;" +
        "uid = sa;pwd = ;database = Northwind; integrated security = true");

SqlDataAdapter da = new SqlDataAdapter(
        "Select * from Products", cn);

DataSet ds = new DataSet();
da.Fill(ds, "Products");

foreach(DataRow r in ds.Tables["Products"].Rows)
        {
                Response.Write(r["Productname"] + "<BR>");
        }
```

Modifications to display in an HTML table:

```
SqlConnection cn = new SqlConnection("server = (local)\\NetSDK;" +
        "uid = sa;pwd = ;database = Northwind;integrated security = true");

SqlDataAdapter da = new SqlDataAdapter(
        "Select ProductName from Products", cn);

DataSet ds = new DataSet();
da.Fill(ds, "Products");

string strResultsHolder;
strResultsHolder = "<TABLE BORDER>";
strResultsHolder + = "<tr><th>Product Name</th></tr>";

foreach(DataRow r in ds.Tables["Products"].Rows)
    {
    strResultsHolder + = "<tr>" + "<td>" + r["ProductName"]
                    + "</td>" + "</tr>";
    }
    strResultsHolder + = "</tr>";
Response.Write(strResultsHolder);
```

Modify this example to retrieve two or more fields. Then any string fields required in calculations could be converted to integer or double, used in calculations, and the results displayed.

To create a new MSDE database, use Access 2000 (save as...adp), which can then be read back as OLEDB in a WebForm.

The following example illustrates how VB.NET as a scripting language makes everything easier:

1) Start a new Visual Studio VB.NET program as a ASP.NET application

2) Add a DataGrid to the form

3) Click on Server Explorer, on the database application (Northwind in this case)

4) Double-click on Northwind's tables

5) Drag and drop the "Products" table to the DataGrid in the form.

6) Right-click on "Data" and "Generate Database"

7) Right-click on "Preview Data" and check if the database table is present (i.e., fill the grid with the dataset)

8) Right-click on the DataGrid form control and select Expand Properties

9) Choose the Data Source(Northwind), the Data Member ("Products") and on the key ID field ("ProductId").

10) Double-click on the form and insert the following code in the "Page_Load" subroutine:

```
SqlDataAdapter1.Fill(Dataset11, "Products")
If Not IsPostBack then
    DataGrid1.DataBind()
```

6.5 Lab Assignments

6.5.1   Use the MSDE to setup a WebForm in C# (or VB.NET) to read the Northwind database's table customers, displaying all fields.

6.5.2   Create an Access 2000 database School with table Students:

- student # (999)
- name (15 characters maximum)
- GPA (decimal)

Add in five records and save.

Create a C# (or VB.NET) WebForm and read (using OLEDB) and display all table records. Then delete 2 records (1 there, 1 not there), add 2 records (1 a duplicate, 1 not there), and redisplay the updated table.

6.5.3   Change 4.8.2 to use Jscript in Web Forms.

6.5.4   Change 5.7 to run WebForms with C# or VB.NET.

6.5.5   Modify 5.7.3 to utilize OLEDB in an ASP.NET program.

6.5.6   In WebForms (C# or VB.NET) set up in the form:

- textboxes for Sales & Costs
- validate each textbox for ranges 50.00 - 1000.00
- button to send to WebForm's "code-behind" Sales & Costs, convert them to double, compute Profit by subtracting Costs from Sales, and displaying:
      PROFIT = (value of profit)

6.5.7   Set up an Access 2002 database School with table students (9999, key), name (15 characters maximum), gpa (9.99) with five records.

Set up a WebForm (C# or VB.NET) to:

- display all the records in an HTML table with a header
- delete 2 records (1 there, 1 not there - error)

- add 2 records (1 there - error, 1 not there)
- change the gpa in an existing record
- display all record in an HTML table with a header

6.5.8   Using MSDE, set up a WebForm to read back the
- table products in database Northwind and
- display all the records' Productnames and
- UnitPrices where the UnitPrice exceeds 8.50

6.6 Test Questions

6.6.1:   ADO

-    With an Access database newYear with table Devry, this SQL statement selects only the records with COST exceeding PRICE: SELECT * FROM Devry WHERE PRICE < COST; T or F?

6.6.2:   Which ADO command moves to the record just before the current record: (a) moveNext (b) movePrevious (c) moveFirst (d) moveLast (e) None of the other answers]

6.6.3:   Given database Devry with table Irving, write the SQL command to select only the records with part = 7.

6.6.4:   Which ADO command moves to the last table record?

6.6.5:   Connect to a ODBC database (Food.mdb) with table Meal, and fields: part (number, key) and price (currency). Use a DataGrid control to display the database's contents.

6.6.6:   ASP.NET Recode the ASP labs to use WebForms with your choice of C# or VB.NET. With the Access database, utilize OLEDB instead of ODBC.

6.6.7:   Recode a JavaScript example in an ASP program to use WebForms with your choice of C# or VB.NET as the scripting language.

6.6.8:   ASP.NET utilizes OLEDB-compliant databases—T or F?

6.6.9:   You can run an ASP program under ASP.NET—T or F?

6.6.10:   Utilizing VB.NET as your scripting language in WebForms requires the completion of coding statements with semi-colons T or F?

6.6.11:   Why does C# script in a WebForm run faster than JScript?

6.6.12: ASP.NET program requires a Server to compile and then run them—T or F?

6.6.13: You could use the Microsoft Database Engine (MSDE) for Full Professional use instead of purchasing SQL Server 2000—T or F?

6.6.14: ADO.NET utilizes Windows ODBC-registered databases—T or F?

6.6.15: Write the following SQL commands for database Trial with table EXAMPLES:
(a) display all fields where price is less than 100.00
(b) delete the record with an itemNo of 32
(c) insert two records:

itemNo	Name	Price	Quantity
47	Printer	450.50	6
214	Modem	57.96	4

(d) display only itemId and Name where Price is greater than or equal to 38.25

Chapter 7

Java Server Pages (JSP)

7.0 Objectives

- Call functions in JSP, passing and returning values

- Do Java coding with the <% and %> tags

- Convert strings to numbers

- Validate numeric fields, using Try/Catch blocks

- Read an ODBC-registered Access database utilizing the JDBC-ODBC-Bridge

- Display database rows in HTML table format

7.1 Introduction to JSP

Sun Microsystems developed Java Server Pages (JSP), which use Java as the scripting language. This means:

- You must know Java to use JSP, but you get the full processing power of a computer language

- Your JSP pages (with Java code within as HTML page whose suffix is jsp) is compiled, with compile errors, unlike JavaScript which doesn't compile, terminating the run on an unacceptable coding line).

- ASP is multi-platform, running on Linux and Microsoft Operating systems. Microsoft has announced it will allow Java to run on .NET platform until 2004.

- Java Server Pages require more knowledge on the part of the programmer than using Active Server Pages.

- JSP and ASP do very much the same tasks on the Server, JSP is more efficient but harder to learn, ASP is less efficient but easier to learn.

JSP can only run under JSP-supported Servers. Excellent choices are Jakarta's Tomcat (free) and JRun, using the Apache server (free, running in Windows and Linux). Of course, you require a Java compiler such as Sun Microsystem's JDK kit 1.3.0_02 (downloadable free from: **www.sun.com/downloads**).Use Tomcat for JSP testing, JRun for professional, high-volume work! In Tomcat, save your JSP program at: c:\tomcat\webapps\examples\jsp.

To run, type the following in the browser's header:

http://localhost:8080/examples/jsp/yourname.jsp

7.2 Using Java in JSP

```
<HTML>
<TITLE>Date example</TITLE>
<BODY COLOR = #ffffff>
The time on the server is
<% = new java.util.Date() %>
</BODY>
</HTML>
```

The java function between the <% = and %> tags (as in ASP) returns and displays a date.

You do not identify the scripting language as Java since the Server assumes that because the file has a suffix of ".jsp".

You can also enter direct Java code between the <% and %> tags:

```
<HTML>
<TITLE>Calculation</TITLE>
<BODY>
<%
       int a = 5, b = 7, c; // Java coding

       c = a * b;
       System.out.println("Product =" + c);
%>
</BODY>
</HTML>
```

7.3 Form Passing Data to the Server's JSP Page

The HTML file is saved with the suffix "HTML" and run on the Client (local) computer:

```
<HTML>
<TITLE>HTML to get data</TITLE>
<BODY>
<FORM ACTION = "HTTP://wrchampion.com/Relay2.jsp"
        METHOD = "post">
<INPUT TYPE = "text" NAME = "sales">
<INPUT TYPE = "text" NAME = "costs">
<INPUT TYPE = "submit" NAME = "Submit"
        VALUE = "Compute Profit">
</FORM>
</BODY>
</HTML>
```

Note that the word submit must be in lower-case. Submit sends the data (sales & costs) to the JSP page on the Server.

The JSP page is stored on the Server with the suffix ".jsp":

```
<HTML>
<TITLE>JSP page to compute profit</TITLE>
<BODY>
<%
        String s, c;

    s = request.getParameter("sales"); // gets the data passed from the form
    c = request.getParameter("costs");
%><P>

SALES: <% = s %><BR>
COSTS: <% = c %><P>
PROFIT: <% = Integer.parseInt(s) - Integer.parseInt(c) %>
</BODY>
</HTML>
```

In JSP you convert a string to data with the function Integer.parseInt, whereas in JavaScript you utilize the function parse.Int.

TABLE display is often used for clarity of display:

```
<TABLE BORDER>
<TR>
    <TH>SALES</TH>
    <TH>COSTS</TH>
    <TH>PROFIT</TH>
</TR>
<TR>
    <TD><% = s %></TD>
    <TD><% = c %></TD>
    <TD><% = Integer.parseInt(s) - Integer.parseInt(c)
            %></TD>
</TR>
</TABLE>
</BODY>
</HTML>
```

7.4 Validating Numeric Fields

Utilize "catch" to discover a failed data conversion:

```
import javax.swing.*;
public class validate
{
    public static void main (String args[ ])
    {
        String    anumber;
        int       number9;

        anumber =
            JOptionPane.showInputDialog ("Key in integer:");
        try {
            number 9 = Integer.parseInt(anumber);
            System.out.println (number9 + " is a valid #");
        }

        catch (NumberFormatException e)
        {
            System.out.println (anumber + " is not numeric");
            number9 = 0;
        }

        System.exit (0);
    }
}
```

The TRY brackets includes statements which may generate errors. The CATCH identifies a specific error (NumberFormat), issuing a suitable error message.

7.5 Reading an Access Database in Java

```
import java.sql.*;
import java.io.*;

class getdata
{
    public static void main (String args[])
    {
      try {
                Class.forName("sun.jdbc.odbc.JdbcOdbcDriver");
                    // for jdk 1.4

                Connection connection = DriverManager.getConnection(
                    "jdbc:odbc:sunny","anonymous","guest");

                Statement statement = connection.createStatement();

                ResultSet columns = statement.executeQuery(
                    "SELECT * FROM Table1"); // SQL statement

                System.out.println("part price");

                while (columns.next())
                {
                    System.out.println(columns.getInt("part") + " " +
columns.getString("price"));
                }
            }

    catch (ClassNotFoundException ex)
    {
            System.out.println("JDBC-ODBC driver not loaded");
            ex.printStackTrace(); // very useful in debugging
            System.exit(1);
    }

    catch (SQLException ex)
    {
```

```
          System.out.println("Unable to connect");
          ex.printStackTrace(); // very useful in debugging
          System.exit(2);
     }
   }
}
```

7.6 Reading an Access Database in JSP using the JDBC-ODBC Bridge

Writing an Access database and registering it with ODBC was covered in Chapter 5 on Active Data Objects (ADO). Java and JSP require an extra connector to the Windows ODBC: a Bridge! The ACCESS database must reside on your Server and be registered there under ODBC.

The following example reads and displays an Access database in JSP:

```
<HTML>
<%@ page import = "java.sql.*" %> // so you can use JCL commands

<BODY>
<%
    Class.forName("sun:jdbc:odbc:JdbcOdbcDriver");
            // for jdk 1.4

    Connection connection = DriverManager.getConnection(
        "jdbc:odbc:MyDB", "anonymous", "guest");

    java.sql.Statement statement = connection.createStatement();

    java.sql.ResultSet columns = statement.executeQuery(
            "SELECT * FROM Products");

    while(columns.next())
      {
        String p = columns.getString("part");
        String pr = columns.getString("price");

        part = <% = p %>
        price = <% = pr %>
      }
%>
</BODY>
</HTML>
```

Displaying the data in a table for clarity:

```
<HTML>
<BODY>
<%
      Class.forName("sun:jdbc:odbc:JdbcOdbcDriver");
      // for jdk 1.4

      java.sql.Connection connection =
          Java.sql.DriverManager.getConnection(
          "jdbc:odbc:MyDB", "anonymous", "guest");

      java.sql.Statement statement = connection.createStatement();

      java.sql.ResultSet columns = statement.executeQuery(
          "SELECT * FROM Products");
%>
      <TABLE BORDER>
      <TR>
          <TH>PART</TH>
          <TH>PRICE</TH>
      </TR>
<%
      while(columns.next())
      {
          String p = columns.getString("part");
          String pr = columns.getString("price");
%>
      <TR>
          <TD><% = p %></TD>
          <TD><% = pr %></TD>
      </TR>
      }
<%

,which will be just before  }
</BODY>
</HTML>
```

7.7 Lab Assignments

7.7.1 Finish the following JSP program by displaying the heading and contents of each disk record using a HTML table. Each database record has three string fields: acctno, name, and limit.

```
<HTML>
<BODY>
<% Class.ForName("sun:jdbc:odbcJdbcOdbcDriver");
        // for jdk 1.4

    java.sql.Connection connection =
        "jdbc:odbc:MyFile","anonymous","guest");

    java.sql.Statement statement = connection.createStatement(
        "select * from credit");
%>
```

Create an Access database (or some other ODBC compatible database, such as Microsoft Server or Oracle) named MyFile. The table credit contains five records with acctno, name and limit chosen by you. Save this file and register it in ODBC.

Remember that the database must be registered ODBC on the Server computer.

If all this is on your local computer utilizing Microsoft's Personal WEB Server or IIs (version) 5, store your JSP file in c:\inetpub\wwwroot and run it from your Browser: http://localhost/yourLab.jsp

7.7.2 Given:
```
        <HTML>
        <BODY>
        <%

            // Place Java server-side coding here

        %>
        <FORM name = "Anthony">
        <INPUT TYPE = "text" NAME = "income">
        <INPUT TYPE = "button" NAME = "validateIncome">
        </FORM></BODY></HTML>
```

In Java server-side code:

if income not numeric: issue error message

" " numeric: convert to integer
if number in range 100-299
issue success message
if number not in range
issue error message

7.7.3 Create an Access 2000 (or 2002) database LABWORK with table INVEN-
TORY: part (xx, key), price (xxxxx), quantity (xx). Insert five records.
Register this database in ODBC.

Write a JSP program to read the database (using the JDBC-ODBC-Bridge)
and displaying:

- a heading

- for each record (WHILE-loop):

- compute the extended price by converting quantity to integer, price
- to double, then multiplying the numbers together
- display part, price, quantity and extended price with spaces between
  them
- add extended price to a total (double)

- after loop is completed, display: TOTAL = (value of total)

(b) Alter the SQL to only select records where the numeric quantity exceeds zero.

7.8 Test Questions

7.8.1 Given:

```
<% @LANGUAGE = JavaScript %>
<% var objConn, RS, strConnection;

    objConn = Server.CreateObject("ADODB.Connection");

    strConnection = "DSN = alpha;Database = beta;UID = sa;PSW = ;";
    strConn.Open (strConnection);
    RS = Server.CreateObject("ADODB.RecordSet");
    RS.ActiveConnection = objConn;
    RS = objConn.Execute(
            "select * from kappa where price < 100.00");
%>
<HTML>
<TABLE BORDER>
```

(a)   What is the file name? File's ODBC name? Table name?
(b)   Finish up the coding by displaying the ResultSet in a table
        with a heading:

ID	NAME	PRICE
(integer)	(string)	(double)

7.8.2 In an HTML page the action is:

```
<FORM NAME = "Final"
        ACTION = "http://wrchampion.com/Destiny2.jsp">
```

Is this correct? If not, correct it.

7.8.3 In a JSP page: <HTML>
                     <BODY>

(place values passed - amount & tax - as integer into Iamount & Itax;
multiply Iamount times Itax & display the product)

```
</BODY>
</HTML>
```

7.8.4 You have everything set up to display fields Acct (integer) & Balance (double). Set up a WHILE-loop to read & display all records while adding up a Balance total:

```
double total = 0.00;
boolean devry = rs.next();

while (devry)
{
        (display record fields, add balance to total &
        move to next record)
}
System.out.println ("TOTAL =" + total);
```

7.8.5 Using 2 pages:

(a) HTML page: form with textboxes for price and quantity & a submit button.

(b) JSP page: get values passed and, if numeric, convert price to double and quantity to integer; if either field not numeric, issue re-submit error message & set numeric value to zero; compute amount by multiplying price times quantity & display all fields in HTML (on this JSP page).

7.8.6 Given:
```
<HTML>
<BODY>

</BODY>
</HTML>
```

In the gap, utilize java code (called a "Java scriplet") to: (a) prompt & read in sales, costs and depreciation as strings; (2) convert all three fields to double; (3) compute netIncome (double) by subtracting the numeric values of costs & depreciation from the numeric value of sales; (4) display:

NET PROFIT = (value of the calculation)

Chapter 8

XML

8.0 Objectives

8.1 Introduction to XML

XML stands for Extensible Markup Language. It allows domain-specific tags to be created and used without formally introducing them into HTML. It provides a mechanism for the interchange of structured information on the WEB.

If you want to send an Oracle datafile via Internet from one location to another site utilizing Microsoft's SQL Server, they have different formats. The Oracle file must be converted to XML and then transmitted to the other site. At the other location the XML would be recognized and converted to a SQL Server file correctly.

XML uses Unicode, each character using two bytes. Unicode is universal, representing many different languages such as English and Chinese. XML is for information, whereas HTML is for documents.

XML is designed to be: - designed for Internet protocols
                         - support a wide range of applications
                         - compatible with SGML (Standard Generalized
                           Markup Language()
                         - easy-to-write programs which process XML documents
                         - optional features are minimal
                         - humanly legible and reasonably clear
                         - XML design should prepared quickly
                         - The design of XML should be formal and precise
                         - XML documentation should be easy to create
                         - Terseness in XML markup is not important
                         - Can store persistent (active) data

This is an introduction to an important area of WEB programming. For professional-level reference I bought Altova's software "xml spy, version 4.3" and often refer to their manual and site at www.xml spy.com.

8.2 Coding Fundamentals

Readability is aided by using meaningful tag names instead of fixed tag names as in HTML. Each tag <NAME> must have an ending tag </NAME>. Comments are enclosed with the tags <!--   -->

The first line must identify an XML document: <?xml version = "1.0"?>

You can create an XML file (name.xml) in Microsoft's NotePad or in Home Site 4.5 (an HTML editor). To check an XML document, open it in Microsoft's XML NotePad (freely downloadable from the Microsoft Internet Site). Loading it into Netscape or Internet Explorer displays the data but does not perform a strict check as XML NotePad does!

You can just code the data with matched tags, indenting recommended:

```
<?xml version = "1.0"?>
<workers>
    <programmer id = "A1234">
            <name>
                <first>Bob</first>
                <last>Heyward</last>
            </name>
            <job>Java Programmer</job>
    </programmer>

    <programmer id = "B6789">
            <name>
                <first>Mary</first>
                <last>Poppins</last>
            </name>
            <job>Systems Analyst</job>
    </programmer>
</workers>
```

NOTES: - workers is the filename (actually workers.xml)
           - programmer is the record name (two are in this example)
           - the id is a key distinguishing one programmer from another (and must contain at least one letter)
           - if programmer is 01 level, name & job are 05, first & last are 10

To get programmer control, a DTD (document type definition) must start after the heading line <?xml version = "1.0"?>

The DTD can direct the XML translation of the data from your database. XML is hierarchical, but can describe a Relational Database also.

If you save this file as mydata.xml and load it into Internet Explorer, you see the tags & data clearly. A plus-sign on the left, means that it will be expanded after it is clicked (i.e., show lower levels of the data). If you click on a minus-sign on the left, lower data levels will be concealed.

Data Type Definition (DTD)

You need some checking mechanism for the data, the **Data Type Definition** (DTD). It must be coded by the programmer, but it can direct the translation of Oracle data into Unicode XML.

A DTD defines the structure of the content that the XML document will contain. Element occurrences control the characteristics of an element:

> ? indicates the element (or group of elements) may be omitted or occur once

> * indicates that the element may be omitted or appear one or more times

> + indicates an element must appear one or more times

DTD Example with data:

```
<?xml version = "1.0">
<!DOCTYPE employees [
<!ELEMENT workers (programmer+)>
<!ELEMENT programmer (name, job)>
<!ATTLIST programmer id ID #REQUIRED>
<!ELEMENT name (first?, last)>
<!ELEMENT first (#PCDATA)>
<!ELEMENT last (#PCDATA)>
<!ELEMENT job (#PCDATA)>
]>

<workers>
    <programmer id = "A1234">
        <name>
            <first>Bob</first>
            <last>Heyward</last>
        </name>
        <job>Java Programmer</job>
    </programmer>

    <programmer id = "B6789">
        <name>
            <first>Mary</first>
            <last>Poppins</last>
        </name>
        <job>Systems Analyst</job>
    </programmer>
</workers>
```

Microsoft's Access 2002 database has features to facilitate XML use without being required to utilize SQL Server. The data is stored in XML format.

8.3 Access 2002 Exports File in XML

Microsoft's Access 2002 database has been enriched with XML capabilities, and can read/written in SQL Server 2000 format. In the future, database communication will be in XML. Since Access 2000 can **EXPORT** a file in XML format, this gets you into the XML world!

First, create and save Access database MyFile with table Inventory containing five records. Since all XML data is Unicode, all three fields should be in text:

    - part (key, xxxxxxx)
    - name (15-character maximum size)
    - price (xxxxxxxx)

Select File, Export, type in new filename MyFile.xml with a suffix of .xml, click Export, choose to save data and schema, and OK

This XML value reads back the file fine with:

    - Microsoft's XML NotePad (where you see here you have xmins:od, xmins:xsi, and xsi.noNamespaceSchema, in addition to the three data records.

    - Altova's "XML Spy 4.3"

This means that the file is a proper XML file and can be transmitted over the Internet to a site with, say, SQL Server or Oracle. At the destination site, SQL Server (or Oracle) would recognize the XML and convert it to SQL Server's format.

Successful transmission! Now figure how to import an XML file!

8.4 Schemas

This is a newer XML tool, fully supported in VB.NET. The coding is lengthier than DTD coding, but very clear. There are SCHEMA code generators available!

Creating an XML Schema in VB.NET:

- Create a new project in Visual BASIC.NET Applications

- Select "Add New Item" and "XML Schema"

> - Using the Toolbox, drag the Element to the Designer Window, resizing it to hold several items

- Click the "diamond E" in the box and type in your Table name: Students

> - Click inside the box on the first empty row and type an element name studno and select its data type (string) from the pull-down box.

> - Do two more elements (name and gpa) similarly, all string. Your XML file will contain UNICODE data (which is string).

- Save the Schema definition (which resembles a database table).

```
                          | ---- studno

      Student   ----- | ---- name

                          | ----- gpa
```

The actual schema (printed in Microsoft Word):

```
<?xml version = "1.0" encoding = "utf-8"?>

<xs:schema id = "XMLSchema2"
targetNamespace = http://tempuri.org/XMLSchema2.xsd
        elementFormDefault = "qualified"
xmlns = http://tempuri.org/XMLSchema2.xsd
        xmlns = mstns = http://tempuri.org/XMLSchema2.xsd
        xmlns = http://www.w3.org/2001/XMLSchema>

    <xs:element name = "student">
        <xs:complexType>
            <xs:sequence>
                <xs:element name = "studno" type = "xs:string" />
                <xs:element name = "name" type = "xs:string" />
                <xs:element name = "gpa" type = "xs:string" />
            </xs:sequence>
        </xs:complexType>
    <xs:element>
</xs:schema>
```

NOTE: xmlns represents an XML Namespace;

        xs represents an XML schema

Creating an XML Document:

- Select File and "Add New Item"

- Click on the XML File Icon and type in: Student.xml & open it

- Select targetSchema in the Properties window

- Choose XML file from the drop-down list

- Using the Data view, type in two records

You now see:

```
<?xml version = "1.0" encoding = "utf-8"?>

<XMLSchema2 xmlns = http://tempuri.org/XMLSchema2.xsd>

    <student xmlns = http://tempuri.org/XMLSchema2.xsd>
        <stud>123</stud>
        <name>Bob</name>
        <gpa>2.8</gpa>
    </student>

    <student>
        <stud>234</stud>
        <name>Mary</name>
        <gpa>3.4</gpa>
    </student>
<XMLSchema2>
```

Note: xmlns represents namespace

8.5 Lab Assignments

8.5.1 Create a complete XML document with both a DTD and data for three accounts. File is BigDeal. Record is account (required ID).
Fields:
- account name
- address (street & citystatezip)
- telephone (1 or more)
- fax (1, 1 or more)
- country (optional)

Data: - one with 2 telephones, 1 fax, 1 country
- second with no telephone, 2 fax, no country
- third with 5 telephones, no fax, 1 country

8.5.2 The following XML file had errors found by Microsoft XML Notepad; correct them. A suggestion: type up this code, save the XML file and open it in XML Notepad to see how much its error messages help you!

```
<?xml version = "1.0"?>
<!DOCTYPE credit [
<!ELEMENT credit (customers+)>
<!ELEMENT customers (company, address, zip?, telephone+)>
<!ATTLIST customers id ID #REQUIRED>
<!ELEMENT company (#PCDATA)>
<!ELEMENT address (#PCDATA >
<!ELEMENT zip (#PCDATA)>
<!ELEMENT telephone (#PCDATA)>
]>

<credit>
<customers id = "A23">
<company>Acme Brick</company>
<address>Moon crater 400</address>
<zip>91166</zip>
</customers>
<customers>
<address>Valhalla
<ZIP>76543</ZIP>
```

```
<ZIP>12345</ZIP>
<telephone>972-1113333</telephone>
</credit>
```

8.5.3 Given the following DTD (document type definition) code three acceptable records for the file with the following specifications (DTD):

```
<?xml version = "1.0"?>
<!DOCTYPE   inventory [
<!ELEMENT   inventory (item+)>
<!ELEMENT   item (partnum, quantity*, price+)>
<!ATTLIST   item id ID #REQUIRED>
<!ELEMENT   partnum (#PCDATA)>
<!ELEMENT   quantity (#PCDATA >
<!ELEMENT   price (#PCDATA)>
]>
```

Then this out in Microsoft's XML Notepad, freely downloadable
from www.microsoft.com.

8.5.4 Write the XML coding for a DTD and the actual data for two customers.
The data file is named SALES (1 or more customers required).

The fields are:
- id (key, required)
- company (1 required)
- contact (last & first names, first optional)
- bills (1 or more, bill # & amount)
- telephone (1 or more)
- limit (1 required)
- balance (1 required)

Data: A1 Devry Fox   34,   67.89 9729296777   100.00 90.67
      A2 Dodd Poppins, Mary 2,   67.99 2147776666   300.00 270.89

8.5.5 Write the XML coding for a DTD and data for two programmers
- first with first & last names, 2 computer languages, 1 Email
- second with first name, no computer languages, 2 Email

Data file is named programmers
Fields are:
- progid (key, required)
- name (first & last, first optional)
- computer languages (0, 1 or more)
- Email (1 or more)

8.5.6 Set up a DTD to control your data file bigTex. Then add in actual data matching your DTD. Check it out in XML Notepad.

8.5.7 In WebForms using VB.NET, have VB.NET create your XML Schema, add in five records, save and run it.

8.6 Test Questions

8.6.1 Given:
```
<?xml version = "1.0"?>
<project>
    <programmer>
        <numberid>Ben</numberid>
        <skills>
            <language>Java</language>
            <language>XML</language>
            <language>JSP</language>
        </skills>
        <salary>50000</salary>
    </programmer>
</project>
```

(a) Add in two programmers.

(b) Add a DTD with required ID attribute, 1 or more programmers, 1 or more Skills, 1 or more salary. All data is #PCDATA.

(c) Convert your (b) DTD to a XML schema.

8.6.2 Given in DTD: `<name></name>`

Between the tags add first name (1 or more), middle initial (optional) and last name (1 or more).

8.6.3 Create an Access 2002 XML Schema and add five data records. Save and read back in:
- Microsoft XML Notepad
- Internet Explorer (version 5.5 or higher)
- XMP Spy (if available)

Close Access, then re-open it and import it, displaying all records.

Summary

Knowing the fundamentals of HTML, CSS, and JavaScript means you can readily set up a professional-appearing Web site with several HTML pages. You can get a free Web site from the Internet but they can't handle ASP. I rent a web site that handles ASP and ADO for about $30 per month, but I also get my own domain name (about $100)!

Knowing CSS means that you will appreciative the ways you can make your Web Pages better in appearance. Web Masters may use these techniques to efficiently modify their Web Sites weekly! Variety keeps the user's interest!

A knowledge of JavaScript lets you utilize programming techniques within your Web pages, including Client-Server Internet interaction, including the use of databases on the Server.

ASP and ADO will be immediately useful in the Internet environment to do Client-Server interactions, including the use of a Windows database on the Server. Moving up to ASP.NET and ADO.NET is not difficult. Of course, you would want to learn C# or VB.NET to use as a .NET scripting language with compilation.

You are not just Microsoft-oriented! JSP gives you access to a multiplatform operating system environment. In the future, users may utilize both ASP and JSP in the same project, or, at least, in the same company. Examine the discussions on this in Web Services magazines.

XML is used with modern databases to store data, as well as being used to transmit data over The Internet—even on computer mainframes!

All this software can be utilized within DreamWeaver (a popular Web development system). If your company uses this, get a good book on DreamWeaver—and on Flash!

Appendices

The Microsoft scripting language VBScript was moved to this section because it can't be used in ASP.NET. Many users of ASP and ADO want to utilize VBScript for now. Actually the JavaScript and VBScript coding look very similar—but not the same!

Since this is not a book on .NET but involves the use of ASP.NET and ADO.NET, a FAQ (frequently-asked questions) appendix on .NET is included.

Appendix A: VBScript

VBScript was developed by Microsoft to be a scripting language to use in HTML WEB pages. It and JavaScript are the only scripting languages allowed in Active Server Pages (ASP).

VBScript is essentially a subset of Visual BASIC. It has some useful instructions that VB doesn't. VBScript runs only on Internet Explorer and under Winders, but not under .NET.

Example A.1

```
<HTML>
<TITLE>Click a button to do a subroutine</TITLE>
<SCRIPT LANGUAGE = "VBSCRIPT">
sub MONEY_onClick
      alert ("LOTS")
end sub
</SCRIPT>

<BODY>
<FORM>
<INPUT TYPE = "button" NAME = "MONEY"
        VALUE = "Money?">
</FORM>
```

```
</BODY>
</HTML>
```

When you click on the FORM's button, you branch to the VBScript subroutine whose name has the event _onClick appended to the button name (MONEY).

Example A.2

```
<HTML>
<TITLE>Pass data to a subroutine</TITLE>
<SCRIPT LANGUAGE = "VBSCRIPT">
sub MONEY_onClick
    Dim mon
    mon = CInt (Document.MyForm.realMoney.value) * 2
    alert (mon)
end sub
</SCRIPT>

<BODY>
<FORM NAME = "MyForm">
<INPUT TYPE = "text" name = "realMoney"><BR>
<INPUT TYPE = "button" NAME = "MONEY"
        VALUE = "Click me">
</FORM>
</BODY>
</HTML>
```

The value of realMoney can be retrieved as a String in the subroutine with Document.MyForm.realMoney.value. Convert the string to integer (CInt) in order to use it in arithmetic (i.e., multiplying it by 2).

Example A.3

```
<HTML>
<TITLE>Validate data</TITLE>
<SCRIPT LANGUAGE = "VBSCRIPT">
sub MONEY_onClick
    Dim mon, mon2
    mon = Document.MyForm.realMoney.value

    if not (isNumeric(mon)) then
        alert "Invalid #")
    else

        mon2 = 2 * CInt(mon)
    alert "New amount is" & mon2
    end if
end sub
</SCRIPT>

<BODY>
<FORM NAME = "MyForm">
<INPUT TYPE = "text" name = "realMoney"><BR>
<INPUT TYPE = "button" NAME = "MONEY"
        VALUE = "Click me">
</FORM>
</BODY>
</HTML>
```

Example A.4

```
<HTML>
<TITLE>Validate data & check numeric range</TITLE>
<SCRIPT LANGUAGE = "VBSCRIPT">
sub EVALUATE_onClick
    Dim MyValue

    if isNumeric(Document.MyForm.DATAIN.value) then
        MyValue = CInt(Document.MyForm.DATAIN.value)
        if MyValue > = 30 and MyValue < = 79 then
            MyValue = 5 * MyValue
            alert "New value is" & MyValue
        else
            alert ("Invalid #")
    end if
    else
        alert "Not numeric"
    end if
end sub
</SCRIPT>

<BODY>
<FORM NAME = "MyForm">
<INPUT TYPE = "text" name = "DATAIN" value = "45"><BR>
<INPUT TYPE = "button" NAME = "EVALUATE"
    VALUE = "Evaluate">
</FORM>
</BODY>
</HTML>
```

Example A.5

```
<HTML>
<TITLE>Select case</TITLE>
<SCRIPT LANGUAGE = "VBSCRIPT">
sub CheckIt_onClick
    Dim k, m
```

```
k = MyForm.DATAIN.Value
alert "Passed value is" & k
if isNumeric(k) then
    Select Case (k)
        Case vbInteger
            m = CInt(k)
        Case vbSingle
            m = CSgl(k)
        Case vbDouble
            m = CDbl(k)
        Case vbNull
            MsgBox "No value"
            m = 0
        End Select
    else alert "Not numeric"
    alert k & " " & m
end sub
</SCRIPT>

<BODY>
<FORM NAME = "MyForm">
<INPUT TYPE = "text" name = "DATAIN" value = "45"><BR>
<INPUT TYPE = "button" NAME = "CheckIt"
    VALUE = "Evaluate">
</FORM>
</BODY>
</HTML>
```

Example A.6

```
<HTML>
<TITLE>3 buttons</TITLE>
<SCRIPT LANGUAGE = "VBSCRIPT">
sub MyButton1_onClick
    alert "Radio special"
end sub

sub MyButton2_onClick
    alert "TV special"
end sub

sub MyButton3_onClick
    alert "grand piano special"
end sub
</SCRIPT>

<BODY>
<FORM NAME = "MyForm">
<INPUT TYPE = "button" name = "MyButton1" value = "Buy a radio">
<INPUT TYPE = "button" name = "MyButton2" value = "Purchase a TV">
<INPUT TYPE = "button" name = "MyButton3" value = "Take a piano">
</FORM>
</BODY>
</HTML>
```

Example A.7

```
<HTML>
<TITLE>Load array & compute average</TITLE>
<SCRIPT LANGUAGE = "VBSCRIPT">
  Option Explicit
  Dim test(5), subscript, total, anumber, average

  sub MyButton_onClick
      total = 0
      for subscript = 1 to 5
          anumber = prompt("Key in integer")
          test(subscript) = anumber
          total = total + anumber
      next
      average = total / 5
      alert "Average = " & average
end sub
</SCRIPT>

<BODY>
<INPUT TYPE = "button" name = "MyButton" value = "Click me!">
</BODY>
</HTML>
```

Example A.8

```
<HTML>
<TITLE>Load array & compute average</TITLE>
<SCRIPT LANGUAGE = "VBSCRIPT">
  Option Explicit
  Dim myArray
  myArray = Array(10,20,30,40,60,80)

sub cmdButton1_onClick
    Dim myElement, i

    for Each myElement in myArray
        i = i + 1
        if myElement = 40 then
```

```
            alert "Found it at" & i
            Exit for
        next
end sub
</SCRIPT>

<BODY BGCOLOR = "red">
<INPUT TYPE = "button" name = "cmdButton1" value = "Click me">
</BODY>
</HTML>
```

Appendix B: Active Server Pages (ASP) with VBScript

Client-side coding is run on your local computer. This coding should be in VBScript or JavaScript in HTML pages. Utilizing Server-side coding requires a site to run on. You take the HTML loaded with scripting code (saved as yourlab.asp) and transfer it to the site, usually with FTP (file transfer).

Example:

```
<HTML>
<BODY>
Please provide your information:
<FORM NAME = "MyForm" ACTION =
     "HTTP://wrchampion.com/yourlab.asp"
        METHOD = "GET">
Price: <INPUT TYPE = "long" NAME = "Price"><BR>
Mailin: <INPUT TYPE = "long" NAME = "Mailin"><BR>
<INPUT TYPE = "submit" VALUE = "SUBMIT"
        NAME = "Compute Charge">
</FORM>
</BODY>
</HTML>
```

Notes: Line 4: This is where you branch to the Internet when the ACTION is activated by clicking the SUBMIT button.

Line 5: GET requests sent to the Server, such data (MONEY) from the FORM appended to the submitting command:

HTTP://champion.com/yourlab.asp&Money = 12.45

Alternatively you could use the Microsoft "Personal WEB Server" (PWS) on your local computer as the Server. In this case, save your ASP file at c:\inetpub\wwwroot and run in Internet explorer with http://127.0.0.1/MyFile.asp

Line 8: This clicked button submits the FORM's data to

wrchampion.com/yourlab.

Sample ASP Page:

```
<% @LANGUAGE = "vbscript" %>
<%
    Option Explicit
    Dim Price, Mailin
    Response.Expires = 0
    Price = Request.QueryString("Price")
    Mailin = Request.QueryString("Mailin")
%>
<HTML>
<BODY>
The site has retrieved the form data:<BR><BR>
Price: <% = Price %><BR>
Mailin: <% = Mailin %><P>
Total: <% = CInt(Price) + CInt(Mailin) %>
</BODY>
</HTML>
```

NOTES: Line 1: Identify the scripting language on the first line of the ASP page. Any coding between the <% %> tags is only processed on the Server.

Line 3: "Option Explicit' requires all following variables to be identified with the Dim statement - but with the data type unspecified.

Line 6: Request.QueryString obtains the character string passed from the Client (local) site.

Line 12: Uses a tag expression <% = %> to display a value. It can contain calculations but the variables used in calculations must be numeric (CInt converts a string to integer)

Run the HTML pages in a browser on your local computer. Key in requested data and submit this to the SERVER ASP page by clicking the SUBMIT button.

Before running your ASP pages on a browser, they must first be sent to the Server (wrchampion.com) by FTP (file transfer):

- go to DOS prompt & type ftp (following by clicking the Enter key)
- type: open (& Enter)
- type: wrchampion.com (& Enter)
- name is: chesslopez & password is: bill123
- type: send (& Enter)
- type: a:/yourlab.asp (& Enter)
- check screen for confirmation

Run Internet Explorer, FILE, Open, select your local HTML page & run. Netscape doesn't support VBScript. Note that you require your own site name, user id, and password.

You could have all this together in the ASP page (which will be FTPed to the Server site):

```
<% @LANGUAGE = "vbscript" %>
<%
     Option Explicit
     Dim Price, Mailin
     Response.Expires = 0
     If Not isEmpty(Request.QueryString("Price")) then
         Price = Request.QueryString("Price")
         Mailin = Request.QueryString("Mailin")
%>
<HTML>
<BODY>
The site has retrieved the form data:<BR><BR>
Price: <% = Price %><BR>
Mailin: <% = Mailin %><P>
Total: <% = CInt(Price) + CInt(Mailin) %>
</BODY>
</HTML>
<% else %>
<HTML>
<BODY>
Please provide your information:
<FORM NAME = "MyForm" ACTION =
"HTTP://wrchampion.com/yourlab.asp"
         METHOD = "GET">
Price: <INPUT TYPE = "long" NAME = "Price"><BR>
```

Mailin: <INPUT TYPE = "long" NAME = "Mailin">
<INPUT TYPE = "submit" VALUE = "SUBMIT" NAME = "Compute Charge">
</FORM>
</BODY>
</HTML>
<% End If %>

Using an Access Database in ASP:

This is facilitated by Microsoft's Active Data Objects (ADO) with Open Database Connectivity (ODBC).

First, create a database and tables utilizing Access 2000 (or another other ODBC compliant database, such as Oracle).

Second, register this database in ODBC:

- Select Start, Settings & Control Panel
- Open ODBC by double-clicking its icon
- Choose System DSN & Add (for a new System data source)
- Select the Microsoft Access Driver (*.mdb) & click Finish
- Type in the Data Source Name (DSN) & click Select
- Select the database & click OK
- Close ODBC

Reading an Access Database (in an ASP program):

```
<% @LANGUAGE = "vbscript" %>
<% Option Explicit
  Response.Expires = 0
  Dim objConn, objRS, strQuery
  Dim strConnection

  Set objConn = Server.CreateObject("ADODB.Connection")
  strConnection = "DSN = MyDB; Database = MyDB;"
  strConnection = strConnection & "UID = sa;PWD = ;"
  objConn.Open strConnection
  strQuery = "SELECT part, price FROM Products"
  strQuery = strQuery & "ORDER by price"
  Set objRS = objConn.Execute(strQuery)
%>
<HTML>
<BODY>
Products:<BR><BR>
<% while not objRS.EOF
      Response.Write objRS("part" & " " &
          formatCurrency(objRS("price")) &)<BR>"
      objRs.MoveNext
    wend

  objRS.close
  ojConn.close
  Set objRS = Nothing
  Set objConn = Nothing
%>
</BODY>
</HTML>
```

Creating an ASP page in Front Page 2000 Using the NorthWinds Access Database:

1) Select File, New & Web
2) Store the new Personal Web in: c:\temp\webtest & click OK
3) Place your HTML & VBScript code on the page & save as mypage.asp
4) Choose Insert, Database & Results
5) Select "Use a sample database connectivity" (NorthWinds) & click Next

6) Choose the desired table from the pull-down menu under the record source (Products) & click Next
7) Select Next if all fields are wanted
8) Select Next & Finish
9) Select File & Save as mypage.asp
10) Click File & Publish Web
11) Browse to c:\inetpub\wwwroot & click Publish
12) Reply Yes to all
13) Select "Let Front Page make the changes"
14) Choose Continue & Done
15) To run, get Internet Explorer on the screen & change the HTTP to:

HTTP://localhost/mypage.asp

Challenge: utilize ADO.NET instead of ADO.

Appendix C: FAQ on Microsoft .NET:

1. Is it easy to convert a Visual Basic 6 program to VB.NET?

    No, because VB.NET is a object-oriented language (unlike VB) many new/changed features were made to enable VB.NET to be compiled into Microsoft Intermediate Code. Examples are: (1) an array's first row is 1, not 0; (2) all variable names must have a data type; etc.

2. What does the .NET framework do for the programmer?

    It provides the basic runtime environment and includes Foundation classes. It includes the CLR (Common Language Interface), which runs your code (including the compilations to Microsoft's Intermediate Language (MSIL)).

3. Which is better: Microsoft .NET or Sun Microsystem's JSEE?

    Two fine products; (1) Microsoft .NET is easier to use and a cheaper; (2) Sun's JSEE is a harder to use and more expensive but more efficient, runs under Windows (but not .NET) and Linux.

4. Is XML used in .NET? .NET databases (such as Microsoft's SQL Server and Access 2002) store their data in XML.

5. Why have a special .NET prompt? This lets you run in the .NET environment with access to the .NET libraries and debugging facilities.

6. What are the requirements for a PC to have Visual Studio.NET successfully installed on it?

    You need a PC with a Pentium 450 (or higher) microprocessor, 28 MB of ram, video card capability of 800 by 600, 256 colors, one gigabyte of hard disk space, Windows NT/2000/XP Professional operating system, Microsoft's Internet Information Server IIs (version 5), either Microsoft's SQL Server database or a OLEDB-compliant database (such as Microsoft's Access 2002).

7. How can I get a "free for 60 days" install version of Visual Studio.NET? Many .NET, C# and VB.NET books include this Installation diskette. You could download it from www.microsoft.com/downloads.

8. Can you use JavaScript in WebForms? No, but you can utilize Microsoft's JScript which runs JavaScript code.

9. Can I use a programming language as my scripting language in WebForms? Yes: C# or VB.NET.

10. Can you use all of the MFC in C++.NET as well as in Visual C++ version 6? Yes, as far as I've checked. Graphics and dialogs worked fine.

11. Can you run an ASP.NET program on any Server site? No, the site must use Windows NT/2000/XP professional and have Microsoft's Internet Information Server IIs version 5.

12. Can you use Netscape's Navigator with WebForms? Not recommended; use Internet Explorer 5.0 or higher for full .NET support.

13. Is debugging easier under Visual Studio.NET?

    Yes, it is much more helpful using the Development Studio. An asset is the use of CLR (common language runtime).

14. Is Visual Studio.NET expensive?

    Students and teachers can purchase Visual Studio.NET (includes .NET) from JourneyEd for $100 (plus tax and postage). Companies can purchase it for $500, with a $300 rebate from retailers,

15. Is J# Microsoft's version of Java?

    Yes! It has garbage collection, can run procedurally or in RAD (Rapid Application Development) as in VB.NET's forms, etc.

16. Is learning how to use objects required to work in VB.NET?

    Yes, VB.NET is an object-oriented computer language with polymorphism, true inheritance, delegates, and interfaces.

17. Is C# a easier language to learn than C++?

Yes, for the language fundamentals, with fewer "quarks" than C++ and no pointers. The more advanced functions DELEGATE (indirectly branching) and INTERFACE (simulates multiple inheritance) are type-safe but more abstract.

18. When and where will Visual Studio.NET be installed at DeVry/Dallas?

The target date is Fall, 2003. It would be installed in the main computer lab and, hopefully, in the classroom computers.

19. Is the .NET platform independent? No, currently it must installed on Windows NT/2000/XP Professional.

20. Do I have to switch to ASP.NET under .NET? No, ASP will run under .NET.

21. Do I have to switch from ADO to ADO.NET under .NET? No!

22. How is Microsoft Office affected by .NET? You can register your .NET components with COM to provide backwards compatibility with Microsoft Office and ASP applications.

23. How is C# better than C++?

(1) Has WinForms for Windows programming
(2) Has WebForms for ASP.NET programming
(3) Doesn't use pointers
(4) Type-safe with managed C# code
(5) Use DELEGATE for indirect addressing
(6) No multiple inheritance (but INTERFACE can be a typesafe "work-around").

24. What computer language is Visual Studio.NET coded in? C#

25. In Visual Studio.NET you can use the programming languages C#, VB.NET and J#? Other languages are available from their providers, such as Eiffel, Fujitsu COBOL, Perl, Fortran, Oberon, Pascal, Python, SmallTalk, etc. But not Sun's Java.

26. Can Oracle databases be used with .NET? Yes, utilizing OLEDB connectivity.

27. Can Microsoft Access 2002 work with XML? Many XML functions have been incorporated: (1) it can generate an XML Schema; (2) you can import and export XML data files.

28. Is it true that Visual Basic arrays start with row 0, VB.NET's with 1? Yes!

29. What happened to Microsoft's Visual Interdev 6? It was incorporated into .NET.

30. Do you have to use Internet Explorer (version 5 or higher) as your Internet browser in .NET? Its use is recommended because it supports the .NET features.

31. Why move from ASP to ASP.NET?

    (1) Can use C# and VB.NET as scripting languages in WebForms, because compiled code runs faster)
    (2) Access to the ease of use of WebForms
    (3) Full support of XML, CSS and other .NET standards
    (4) Access to the .NET platform extending the Windows API
    (5) Built-in security from the Windows Server
    (6) Integrates with ADO.NET for database access

32. Why move from ADO to ADO.NET?

    ADO.NET is the latest version of Microsoft's "Active Data Objects", designed to communicate with Microsoft's "Component Object Model" (COM) framework under .NET architecture. SQL Server works well with ADO.NET. Access 2002 (and other Windows databases) can be used through OLEDB (not ODBC as in ADO).

33. Is Java available under .NET?

    J# is one of the Visual Studio.NET languages. Sun Microsystem's Java is not expected to be supported by Microsoft past 2004, ostensibly because Java's "Virtual Computer" is incompatible with .NET (probably true).

34. Is MFC not available in C#? No, it's there and can be called with API calls. WinForms is intended to make Windows Programming easier.

35. Is .NET an operating system? Not yet! It adds the .NET architecture to the Windows (NT/2000/XP Professional) operating systems. In 2003 Microsoft announced that NET was not going to be an operating system.

36. Why was Visual Basic changed to VB.NET?

   All .NET languages must be compiled to Microsoft Intermediate Code. VB had to be "improved" in order to be able to be compilable. In my professional evaluation, this made VB.NET a better computer language. For example, VB.NET is object-oriented and all variables must have a data type.

37. Would a school use Microsoft's .NET Passport? If good student security at the user level is desired! It is a nuisance to register with Microsoft!.

38. Does "COM" vanish in .NET? No, COM/COM+ is the backbone for Microsoft's Distributed Internet Applications (DNA) platform.

39. Is C++ still viable in C++.NET?

   Yes, with the programmer having a choice of utilizing WinForms and/or MFC. It is expected that Microsoft will try to convert C++ users to C# over a period of time.

40. How good is the security in .NET?

   If you use Microsoft's PassPort, probably good at the student level. Visual Studio.NET provides built-in security features so the Administrator can determine who in your system gets access to your C#/VB.NET program code and resources with System.Security and System.Security.Cryptography.

41. Is it difficult to switch from C++ or Java to C#?

   No, the fundamentals are similar but more type-safe. Pointers and multiple inheritance are not available. The more advanced functions DELEGATE (indirect addressing) and INTERFACE (simulates multiple inheritance) are type-safe, resulting in fewer "surprises". The "program flow" of C# is more like Java's than C++'s. There is garbage collection. TRY/CATCH blocks control run errors. WinForms make Windows Programming easy, unlike C++'s MFC!

42. Are Web Services ready for "Prime Time"?

    Microsoft has a SOAP Toolkit allowing the rewriting of remote procedure calls in COM components over HTTP, and having VB.NET and .NET makes it easier to create or use a WEB Service. These services are not completely mature!

43. Is Sun's Forte's IDE comparable to Microsoft's .NET IDE. Yes, and it is excellent, being highly object-oriented!

44. Can you do all of the SWING classes' functionality in C#, VB.NET and/or J#? Yes, for J# with Microsoft's MFC (Windows Foundation Classes). This needs to be checked out in C# and VB.NET.

45. Will there be a Microsoft Office.NET? Microsoft hasn't announced it yet.

46. What is CLR (Common Language Runtime)?

    CLR provides the basic execution services for the .NET Frameworks. Key features include: (1) runtime interactivity; (2) programs can be run without recompiling on any operating system and processor combination that supports the CLR; (3) its ability to analyze MSIL instructions as being safe or unsafe; (4) simplified deployment; (5) an assembly can run properly with new versions of assemblies it depends on without recompiling; (6)cross language integration; (7) interoperability with legacy code.

47. If you had to learn only .NET or Sun's technology (JSEE), which would you learn first?

    If you use Windows operating systems, then I would choose to Learn .NET first. If you use LINUX, then choose JSEE. Both systems are so comprehensive it would be difficult to learn both at the professional level.

48. Should college students be familiar with both C# and VB.NET?

    It would position them well for the growing market. Actually C# and VB.NET compile to very similar MSIL (Microsoft Intermediate Language). Teach WinForms (instead of MFC) in C# and Web Forms in VB.NET and your students will be very Internet-ready.

You could just teach C# with WinForms and WebForms for a similar result. Replacing Java with C# is very viable. VB.NET is easier to use than Java or C#, an important point.

Bibliography

Altova: "XML Spy Suite 4.3", 2002, ISBN 0-595-21902-0,
  - The extensive manual coming with the software, including tutorials

Annunzito & Kaminaris: "JavaServer Pages in 24 Hours", SAMS
  - a fine introductory but inexpensive book

Boumphrey: "XML for Dummies (2nd edition)", Tittel

Bowman: "Visual BASIC.NET", Hungry Minds, 2002,
  ISBN 0-7645-3649-4

Burd: "JSP: JavaServer Pages", by M & T Books

Carey & Kemper: "Creating Web Pages with HTML and XML:",
  Thomson Course Technology, 2003, ISBN 0-619-10115-6

Clark, et al: "VBScript: Programmer's Reference", WROX, 1999,
  ISBN 1-861002-71-8

Evjen: "XML WEB Services for ASP.NET", Wiley, 2002,
  ISBN 0-7645-4929-8

Hatfield: "ASP.NET for Dummies", Hungry Minds, 2002,
  ISBN 0-7645-0866-0

Houghland & Tavistock: "Core JSP", Prentice-Hall

Kaufman, et al: "Beginning ASP.NET Databases Using C#", WROX, 2002,
  ISBN 1-86100-741-8

Liberty: "Programming C#", O'Reilly, 2003, ISBN 0-596-00489-3
  - Excellent examples and explanations; for the self-studier
    (no quizzes or labs);
  - Available on CDROM's from AppDev

Mogha & Bhargava: "Sun ONE Studio Programming", Wiley, 2002,
    ISBN 0-7645-4945-6.

Navarro, White & Burma: "Mastering XML", Sybex
    - a full-sized book for the prospective XML practitioner

Petroutsos, Schongar, et al: "VBScript Unleashed", SAMS.NET
    - an older book with many useful examples

Robinson, et al: "Professional C# (Second Edition)", WROX, 2002,
    ISBN 1-861007-04-3

Seely, Smith & Schaffer: "Creating and Consuming WEB Services in
    "Visual BASIC", Addison-Wesley, 2002, ISBN 0-672-32156-4

Sharp, Landshaw & Roxburgh: "Microsoft J++.NET", Microsoft Press, 2003,
    ISBN 0-7356-1550-0

Thomson, Castro: "HTML for the World Wide WEB", Peachpit Press, 2000,
    ISBN 0-2-1-35434

Troelsen: "C# and the .NET Platform", Appress, 2002,
    ISBN 1-893115-59-3

Whitehead: "Active Pages 3.0", Visual from maranGraphics
    - an excellent visual exposition with concise examples

Wille & Koller: "Active Server Pages in 24 Hours", SAMS
    - a fine, short, inexpensive introduction

Wilton: "Beginning JavaScript", WROX
    - well-written introduction

Winsor & Freeman: "Jumping JavaScript", Sun Microsystems, 1997,
    ISBN 0-13-841941-8

0-595-29731-5